Probability
Model
Masters

Probability Model Masters

◆◆◆◆◆◆◆◆◆◆◆◆◆◆◆◆◆◆◆◆◆

For use in generating and demonstrating random events

by Dale Seymour

Dale Seymour Publications

Order number DS21110
ISBN 0-86651-537-2

1 2 3 4 5 6 7 8 9 10—MA—94 93 92 91 90

DALE
SEYMOUR
PUBLICATIONS
P.O. BOX 10888
PALO ALTO, CA 94303

Contents

◆ ◆ ◆ ◆ ◆ ◆ ◆ ◆ ◆ ◆ ◆ ◆ ◆ ◆ ◆ ◆ ◆ ◆ ◆

Spinner Masters

**Dice, Heads and Tails Cards,
& Color Card Masters**

Introduction

◆ ◆

Everyone should understand the basic concepts of probability. For this reason, the study of probability has become increasingly prevalent at every grade level in our mathematics curriculum.

Teachers usually model or explain the elementary concepts of probability by presenting examples of random events, such as drawing one card from a deck of playing cards, spinning a spinner, rolling dice, or drawing a colored ball from a container. This book is designed to provide teachers with graphic masters that can be used to make overhead transparencies of these common probability models. For example, you can make your own complete deck of transparent playing cards from models in this book.

Because a book of probability model masters would be incomplete without spinner masters, this book also includes the complete contents of a popular teacher resource, *Bases for Transparent Spinners.* Many teachers have used this book on its own for game activities.

What This Book Includes

This book contains transparency masters for playing cards, spinners, dice, heads and tails cards, and color cards (a substitute for the colored balls that are randomly drawn from a box). For all masters except the heads and tails cards, blanks are included so that you may create your own categories. You or your students may use permanent felt-tip pens to decorate or color the transparency graphics. For more permanent and consistent color, you may wish to use colored transparency film, which is available at most art supply stores.

The masters for card decks include two sizes of cards. The standard card deck is featured, as well as circle, triangle, square, and pentagon "suits" that serve as alternatives to the traditional deck. The masters include both solid and outlined versions of each of these shapes; the outlined shapes may be filled in with different colors to customize or vary your deck. The card deck masters include very light markings to assist in trimming the sheet with a paper cutter. You may fine-tune trim or round corners with scissors if desired.

This book also includes a wide variety of spinner masters, which have from 2–10 equal sectors. For each basic type, this book provides one numbered spinner design, one lettered spinner design, and one spinner design with a name of a different color in each sector. In addition, the book includes undivided circles to use for designing your own spinners, and a blank spinner of each size and type for you to designate with your own categories. Use the circular protractor master on page 104 to create spinner designs with other than 2–10 sectors or with various combinations of unequal sectors.

Transparent spinner bases are available from Dale Seymour Publications or other teacher supply outlets. If you expect to use one frequently, you may find it convenient to tape a transparent spinner to a spinner base.

How to Use This Book

The pages of this book were designed to be photocopied on transparency film. Nearly all photocopy machines accept transparency film either in the paper bin or when hand fed. A variety of transparency film materials are available. Since you may wish to shuffle the transparent cards you create, it is best to use heavy film material. Different copy machines may require or recommend different types of transparency film.

You do not need to remove the pages you are copying from the book—just be certain that the page being copied lies flat against the glass of the copy machine. Before using the transparent film, it's a good idea to run sample copies on sheets of blank paper to assure the position, darkness, and quality of the copy.

If you wish to vary the sizes of any of these models, most copy machines provide enlargement or reduction options.

Playing Card Masters

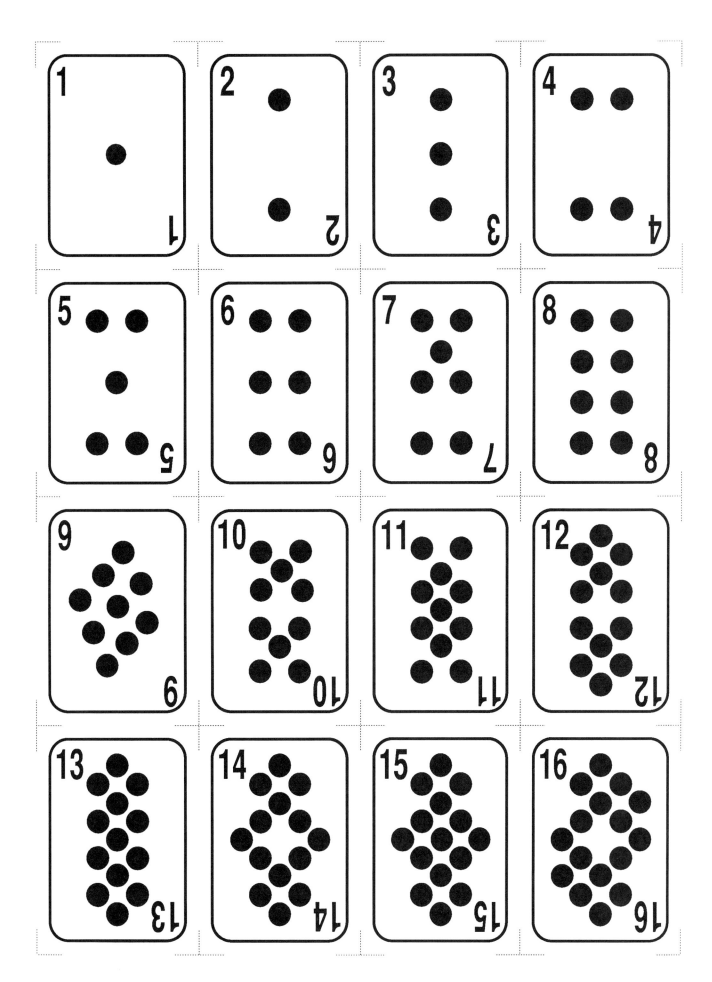

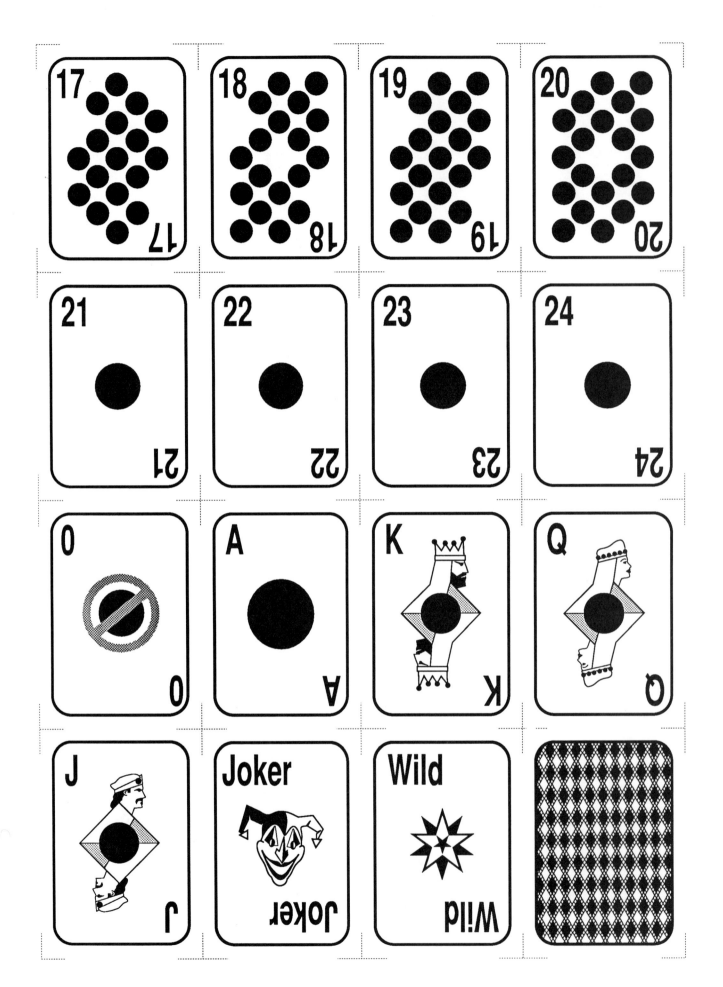

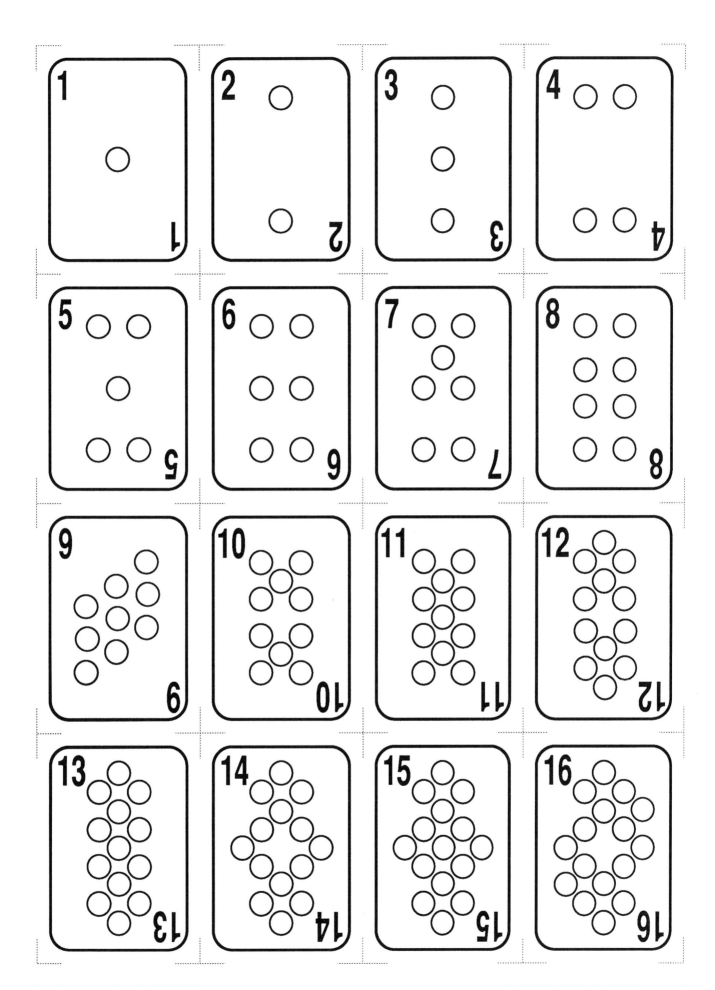

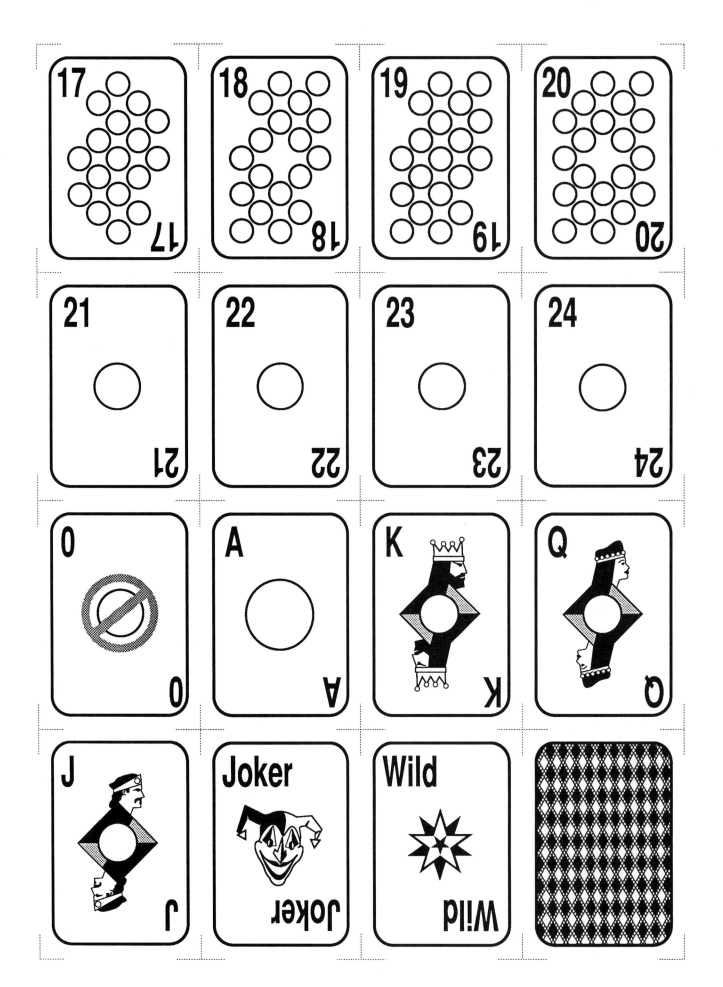

PROBABILITY MODEL MASTERS
© Dale Seymour Publications

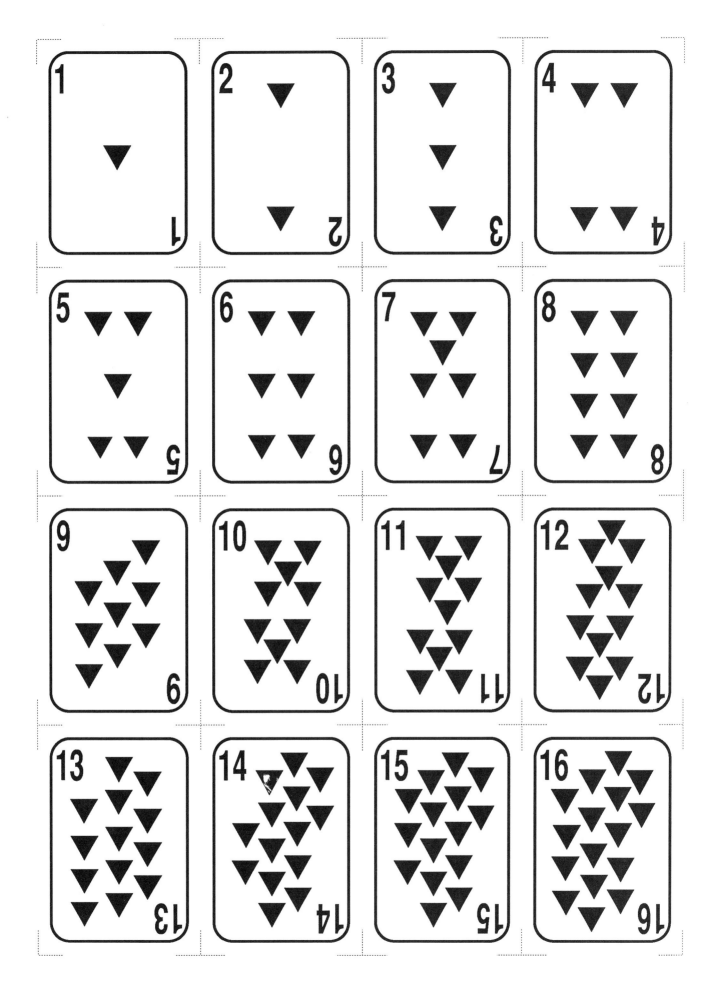

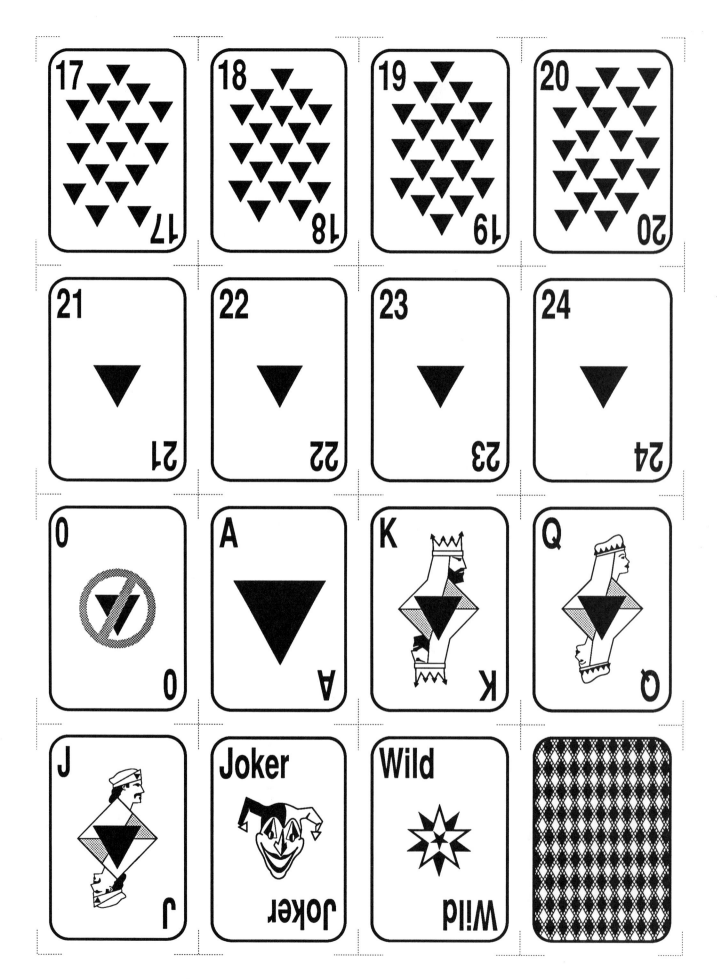

PROBABILITY MODEL MASTERS
© Dale Seymour Publications

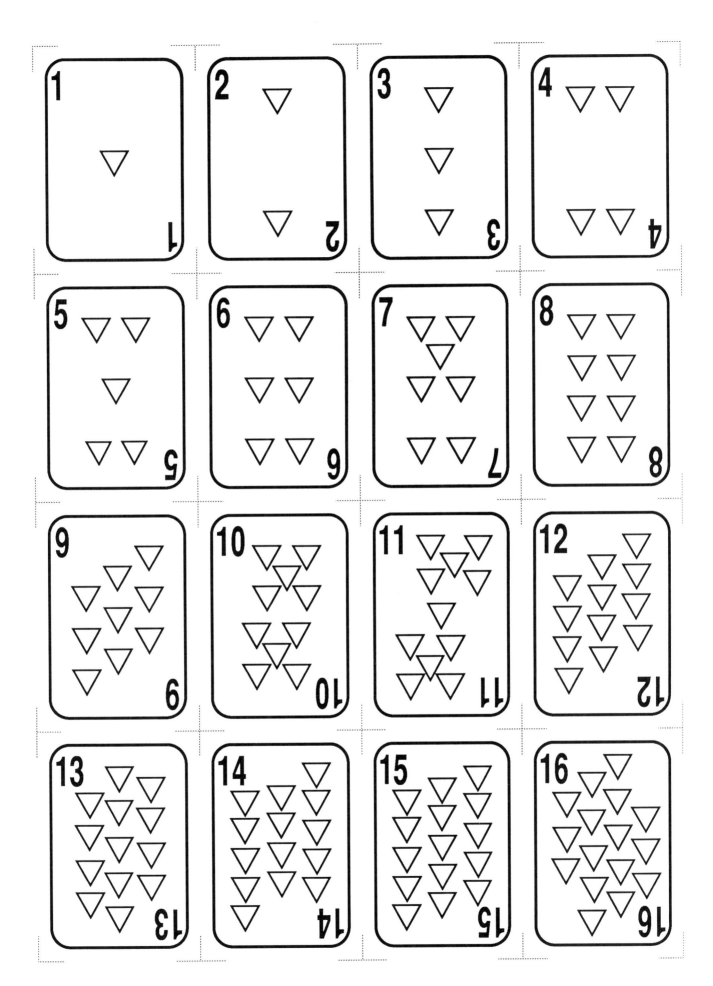

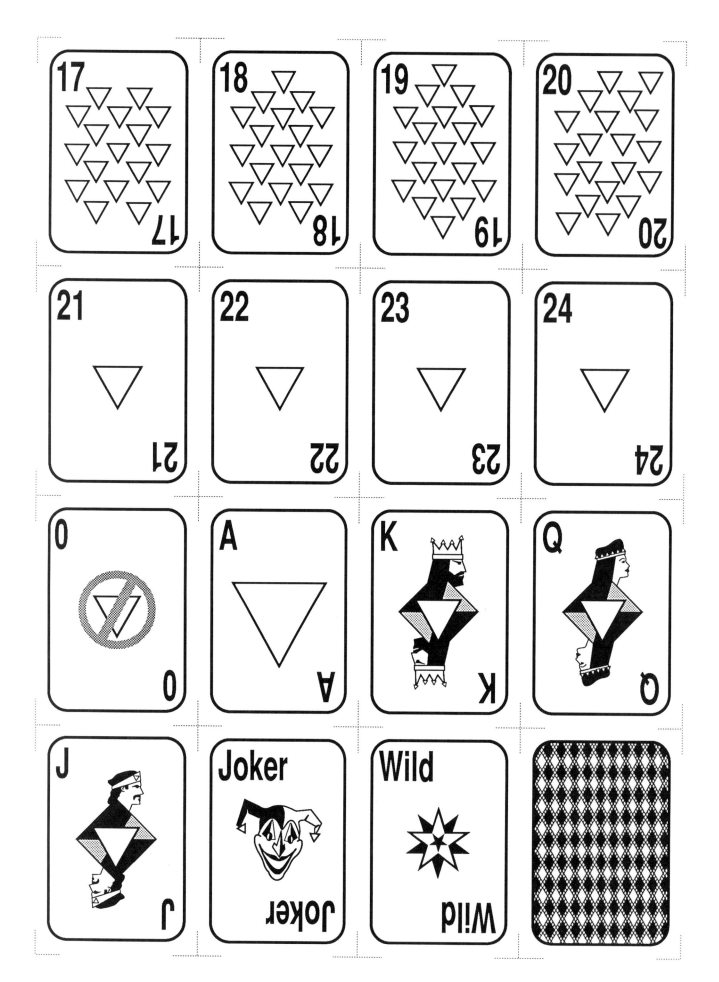

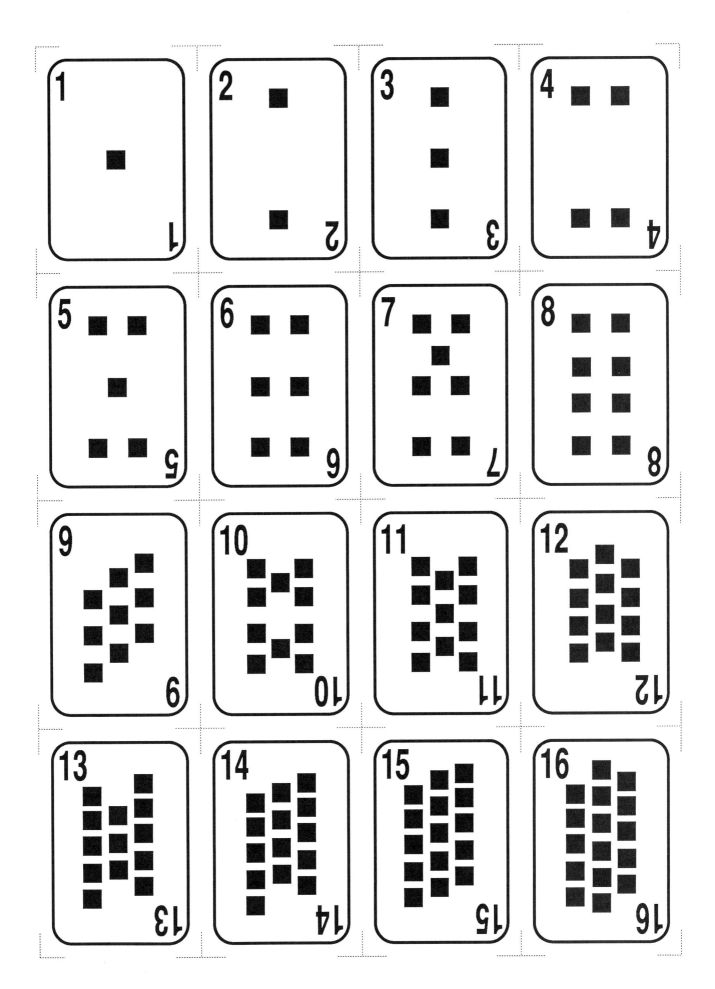

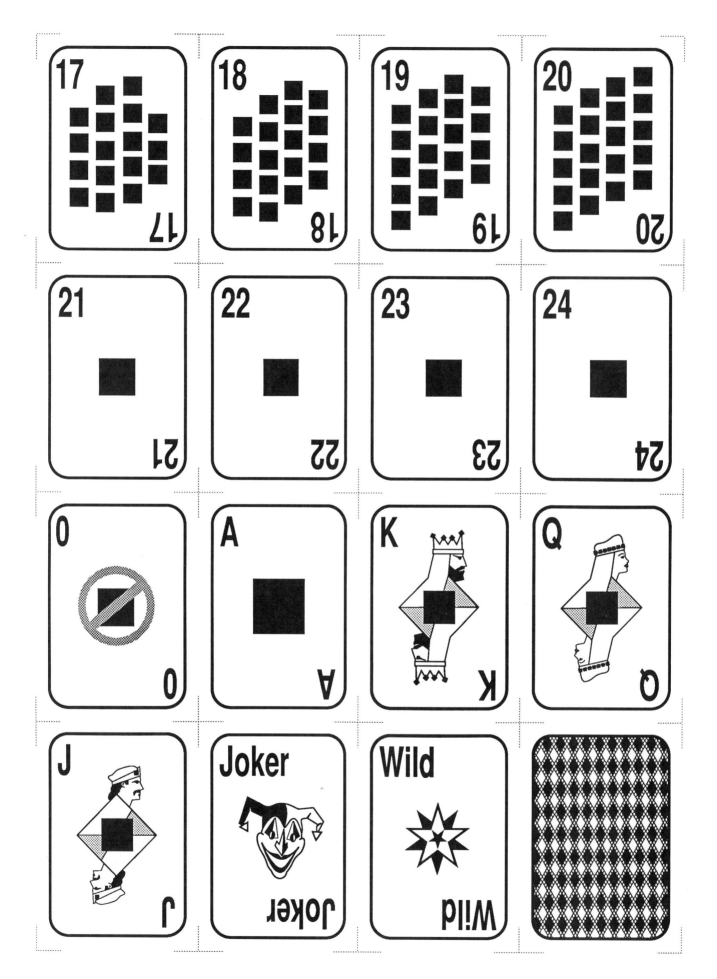

PROBABILITY MODEL MASTERS
© Dale Seymour Publications

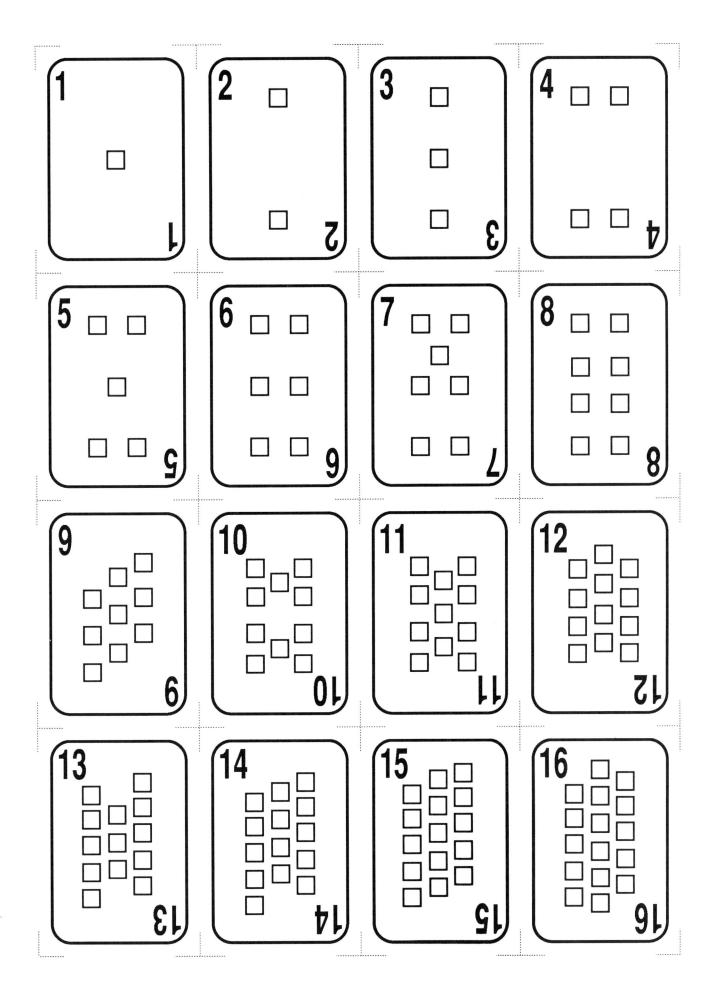

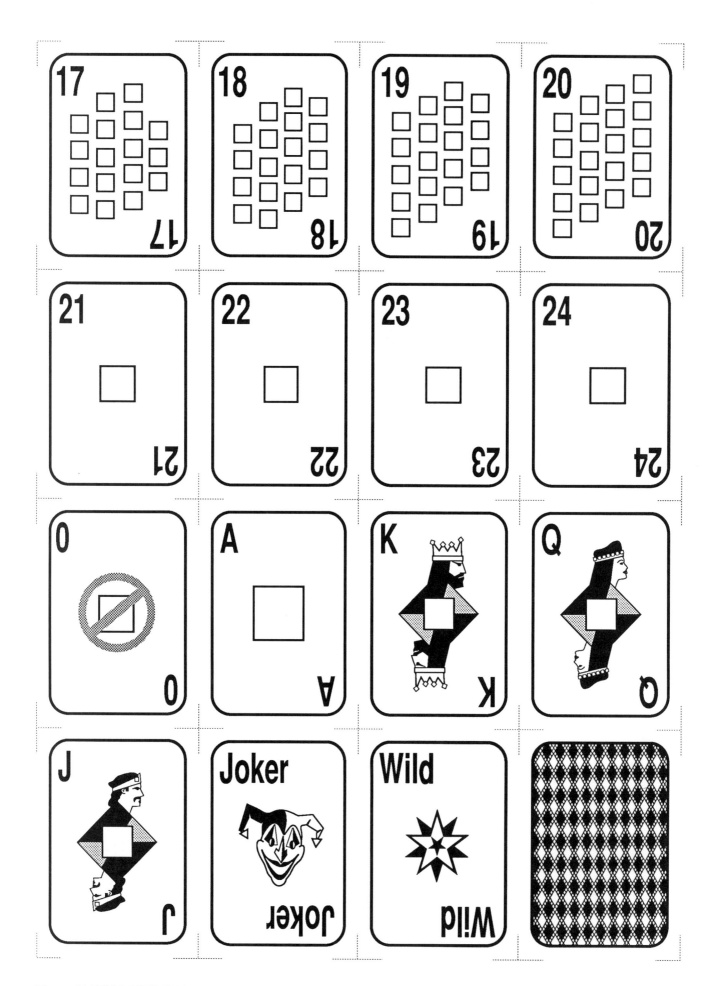

PROBABILITY MODEL MASTERS
© Dale Seymour Publications

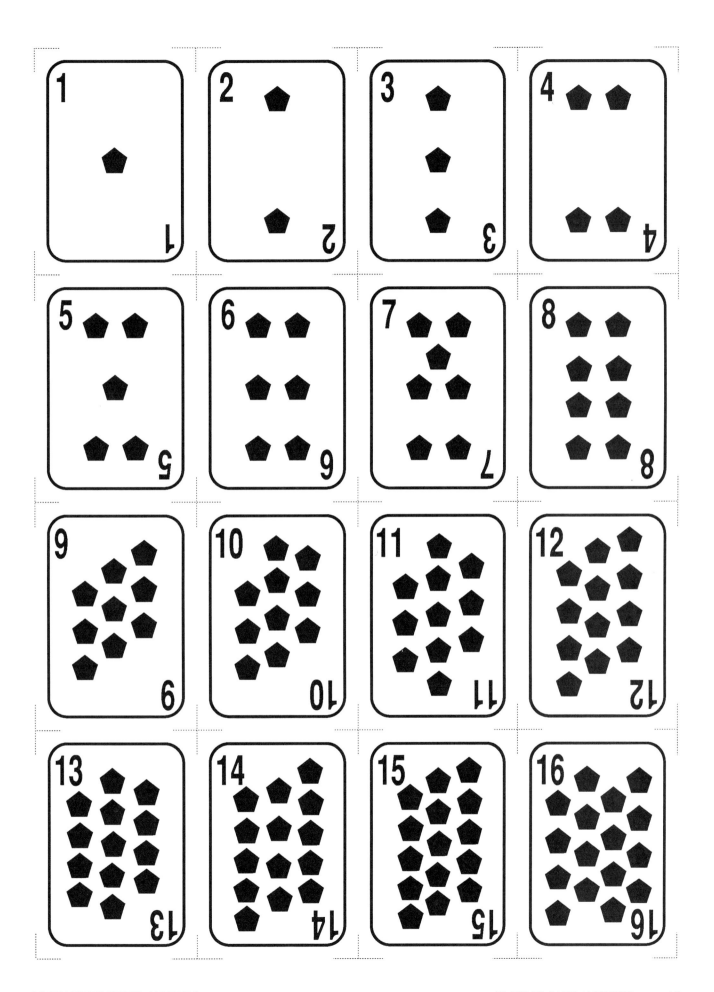

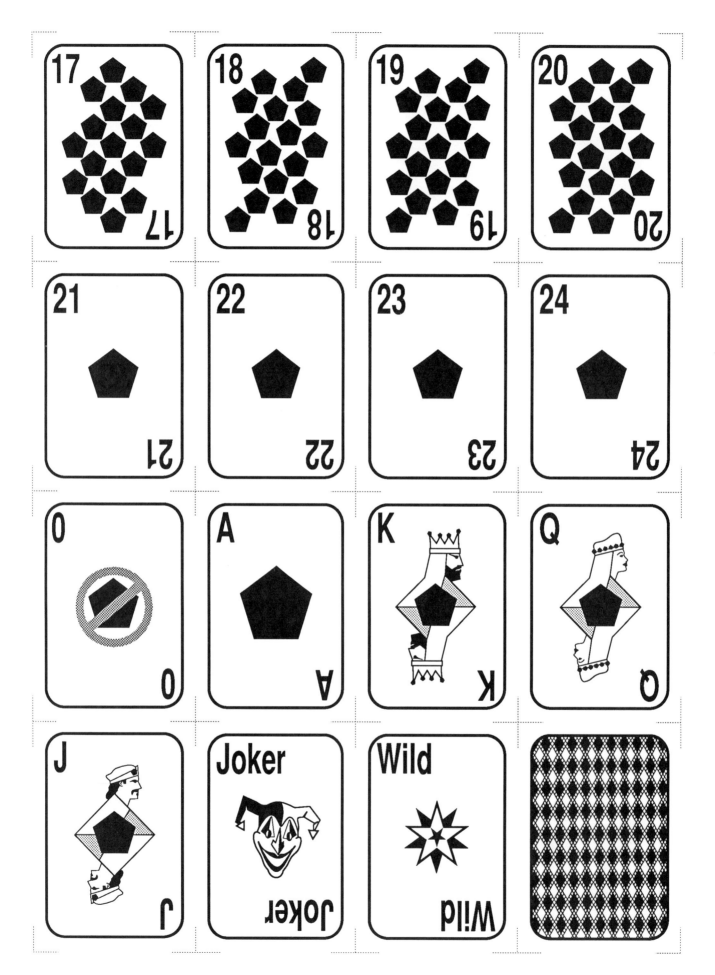

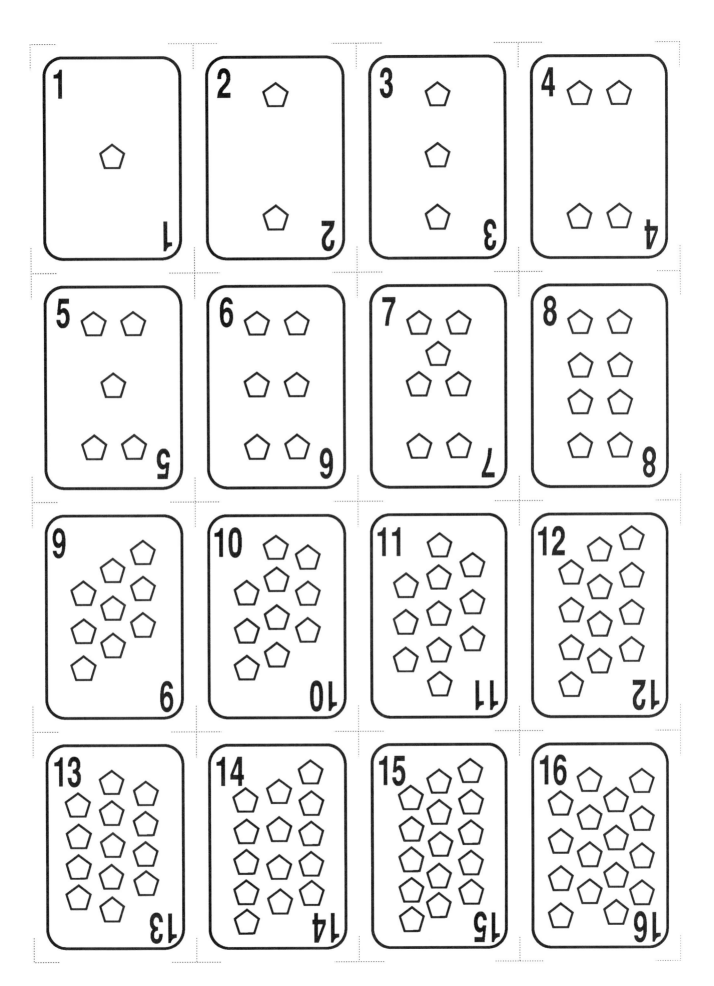

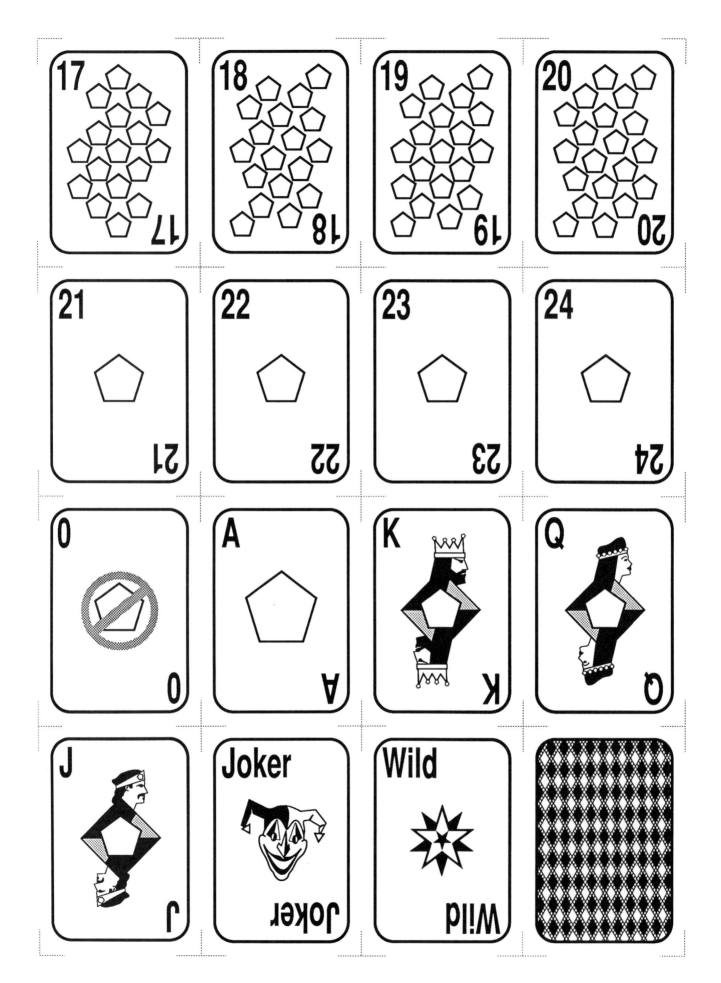

PROBABILITY MODEL MASTERS
© Dale Seymour Publications

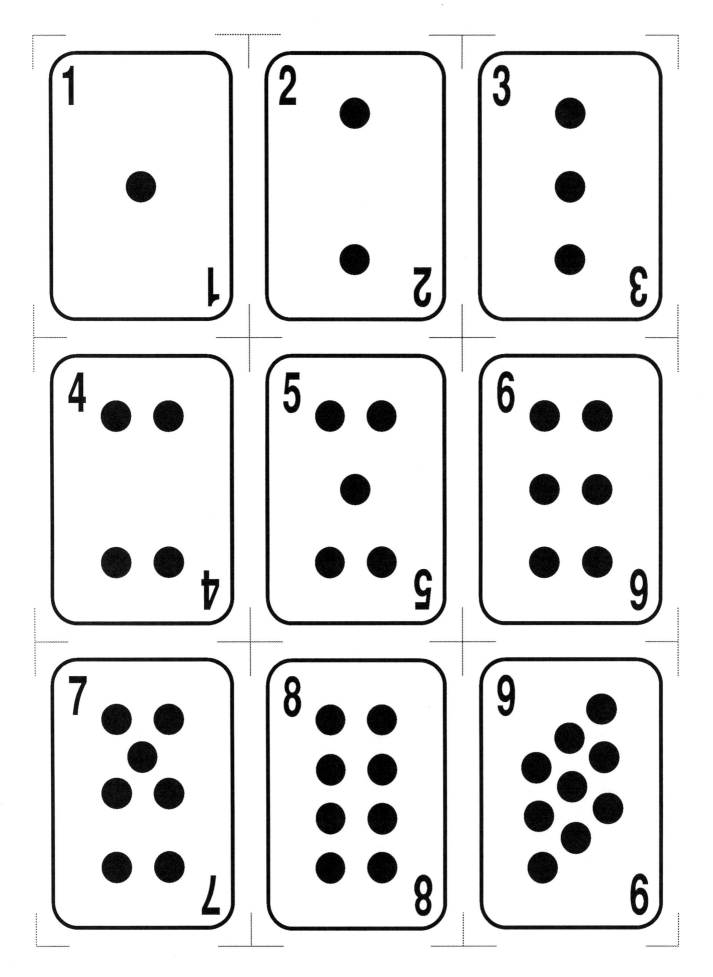

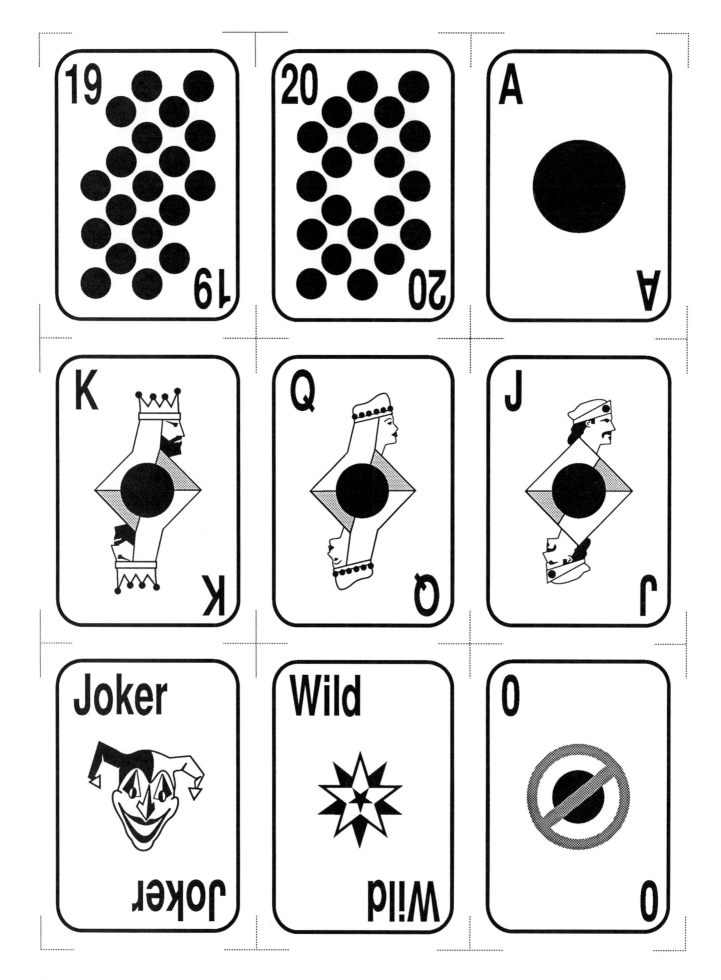

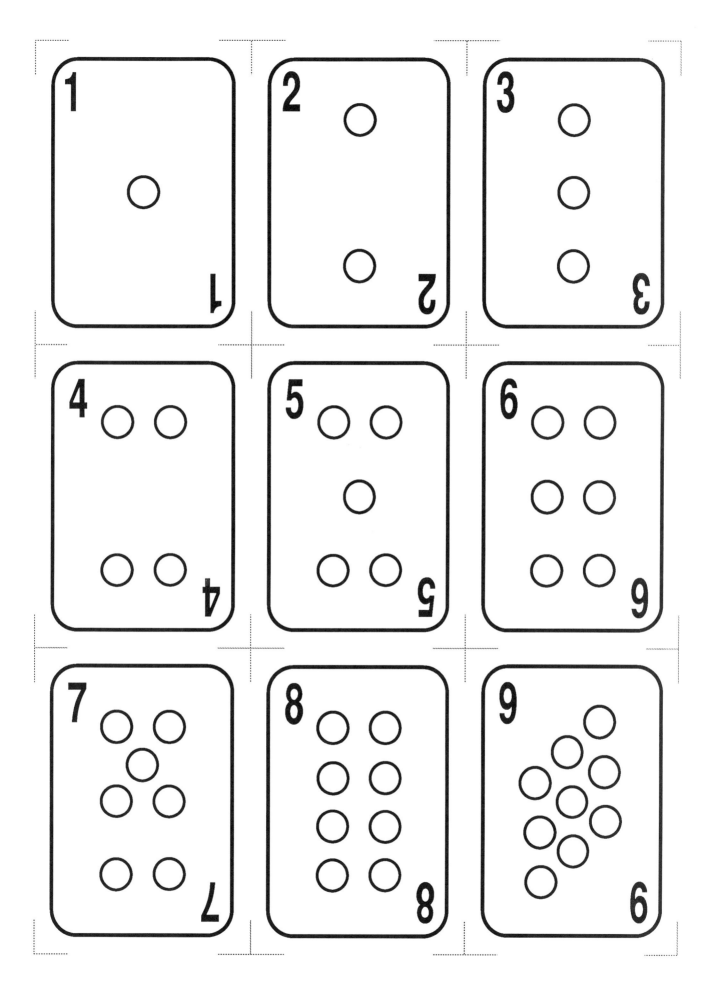

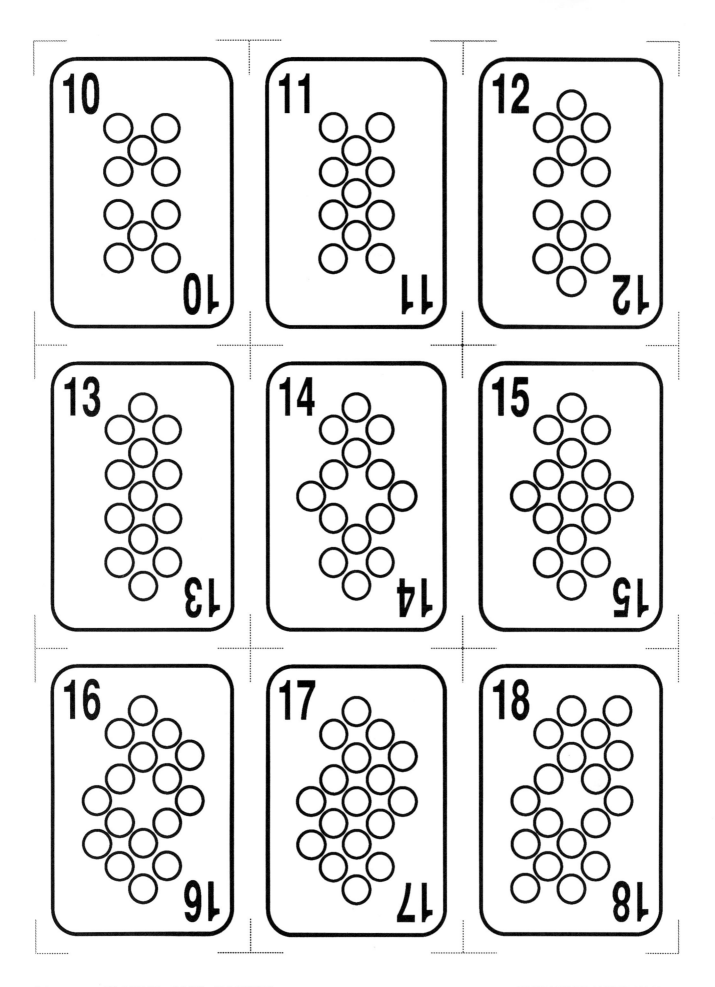

PROBABILITY MODEL MASTERS
© Dale Seymour Publications

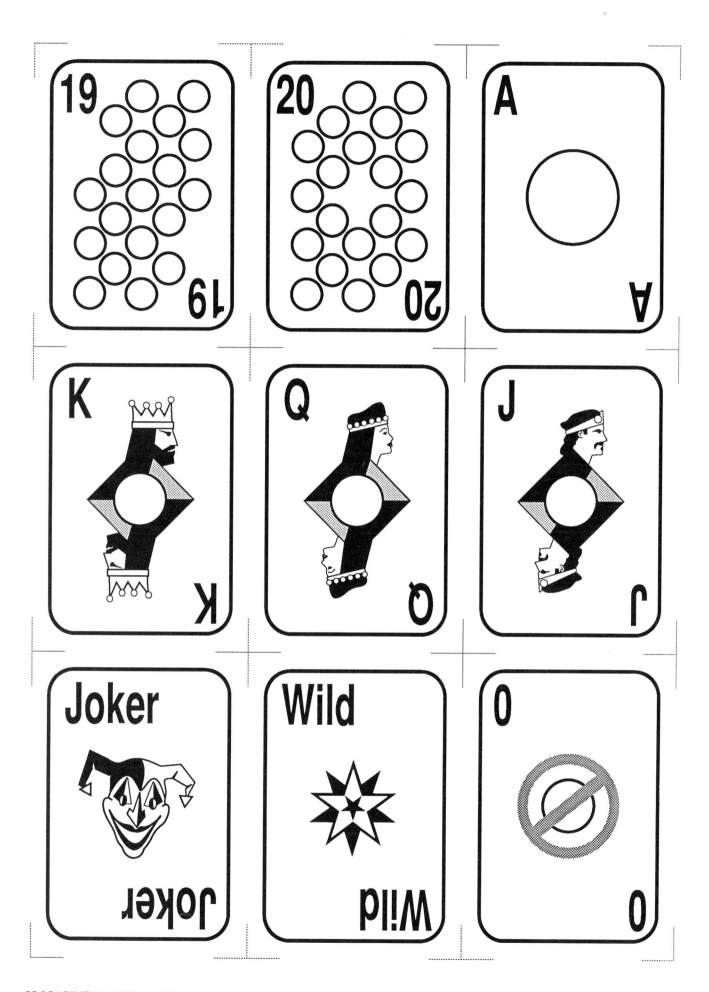

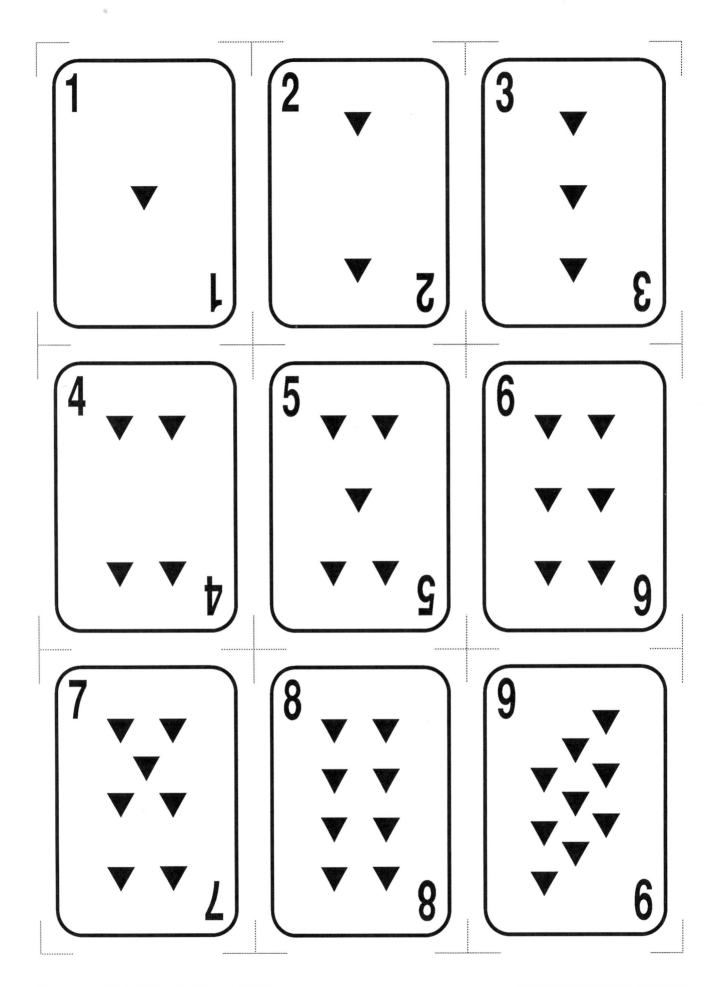

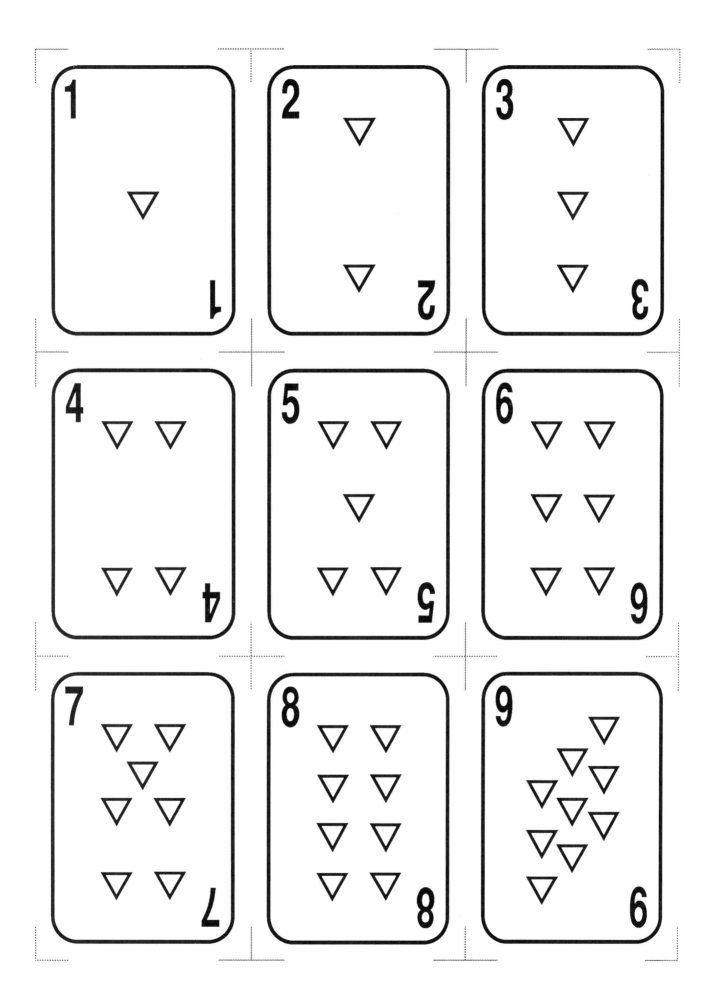

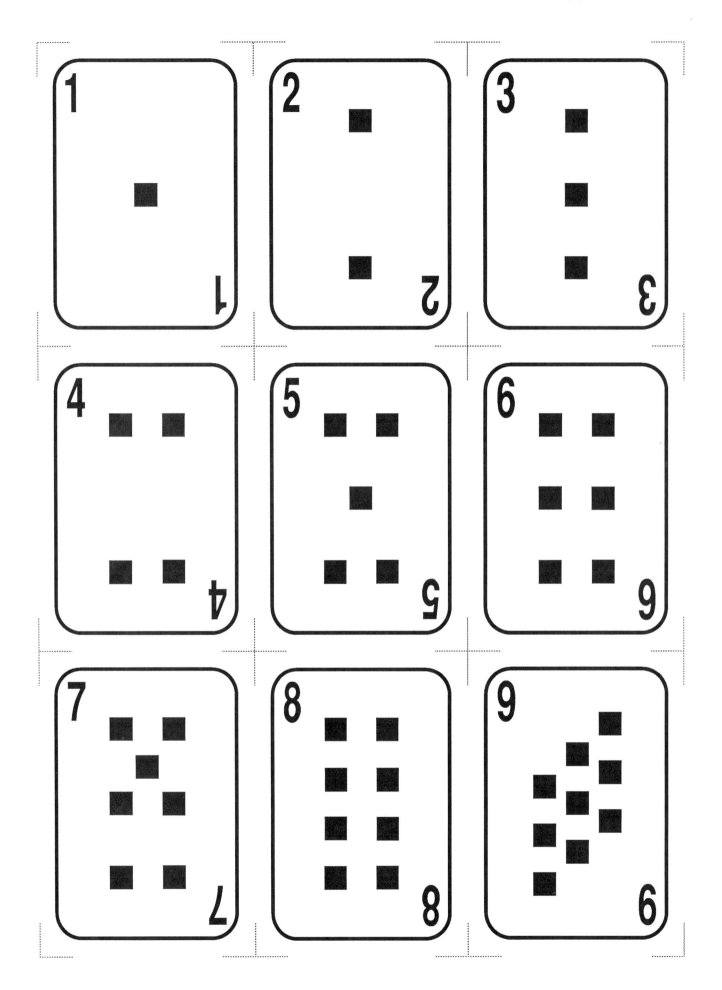

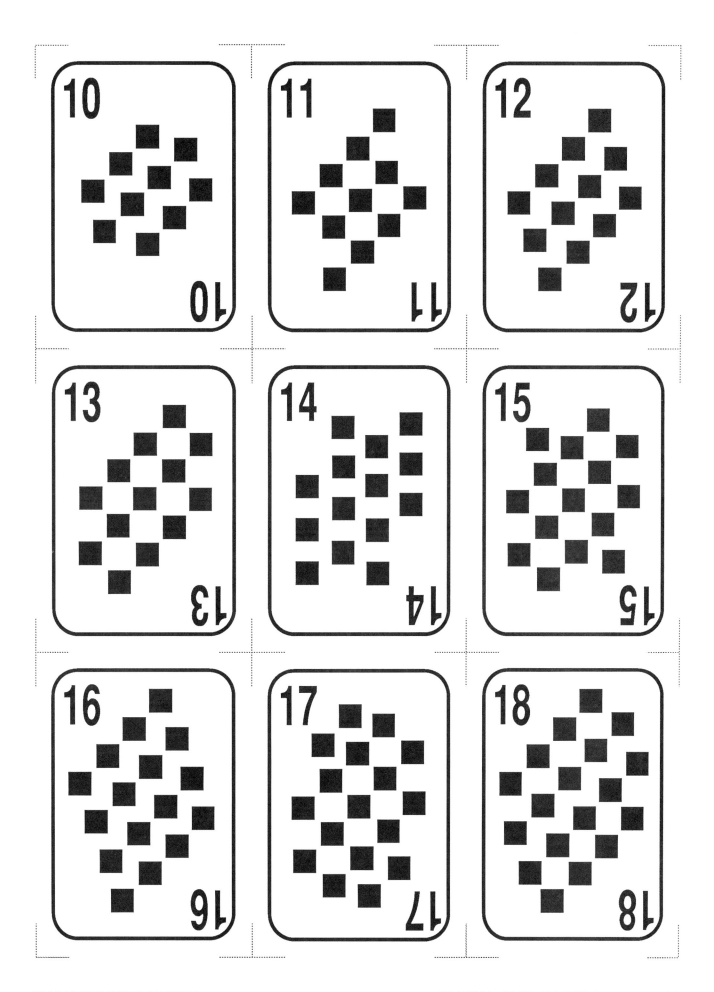

PROBABILITY MODEL MASTERS
© Dale Seymour Publications

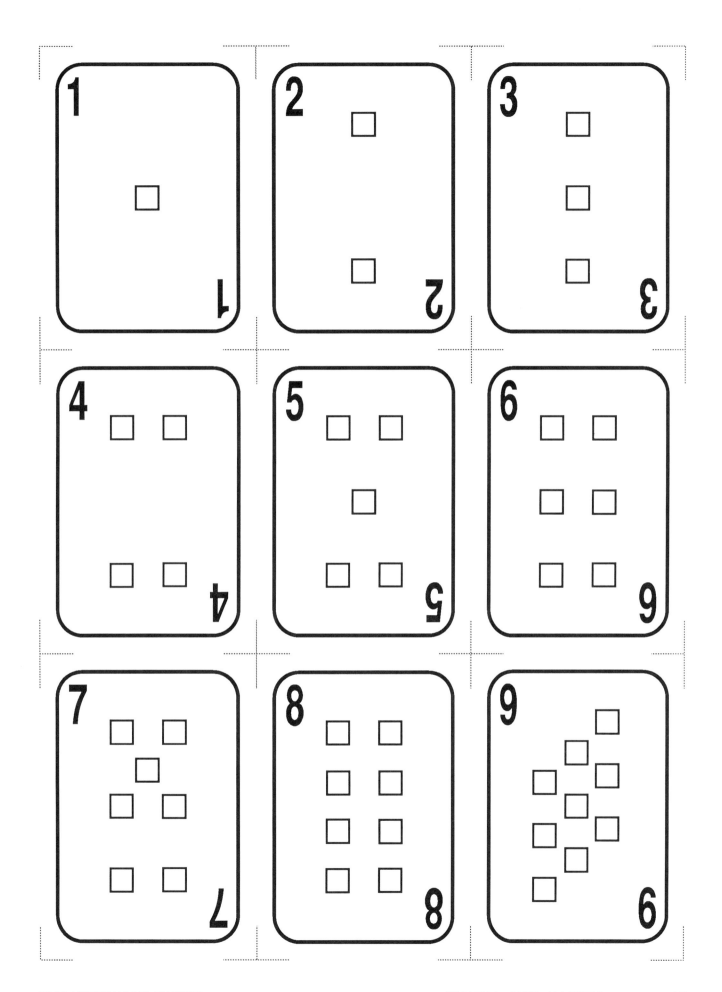

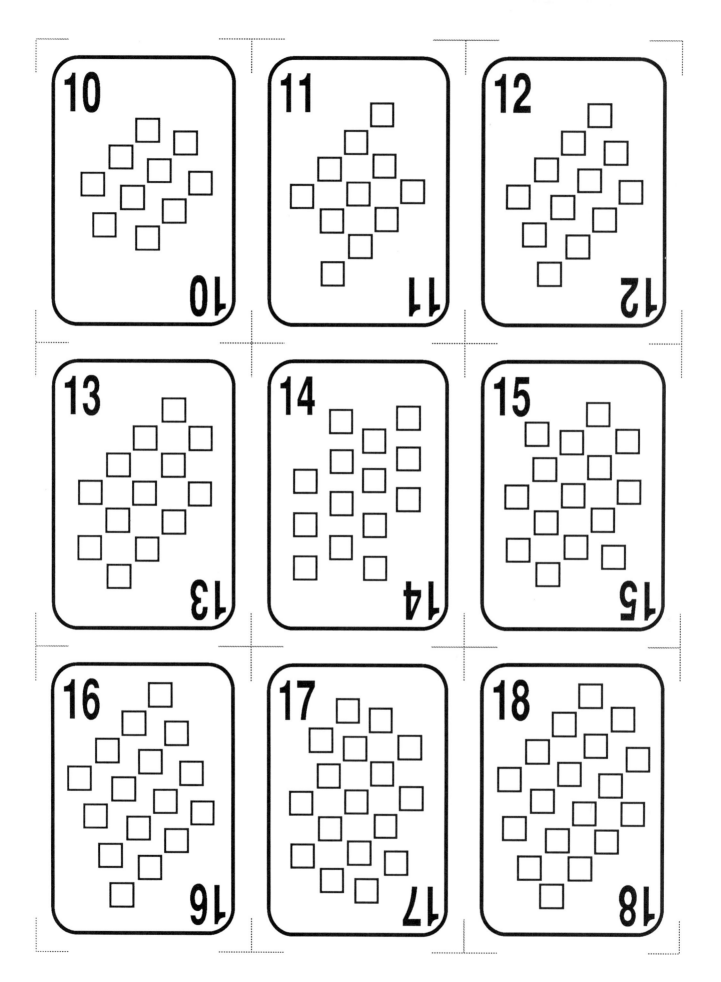

PROBABILITY MODEL MASTERS
© Dale Seymour Publications

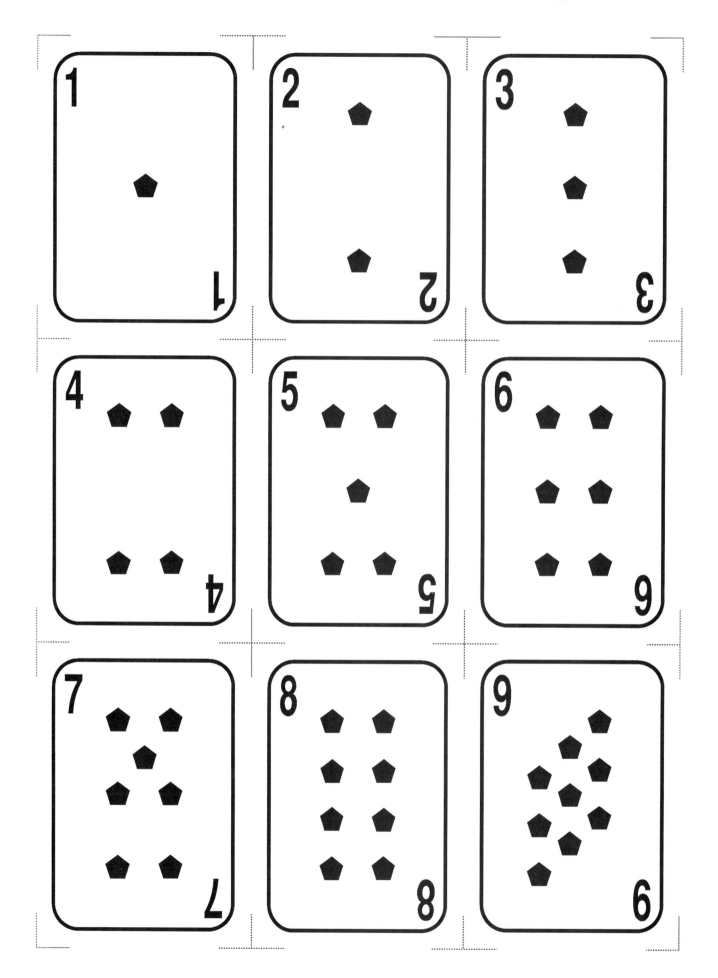

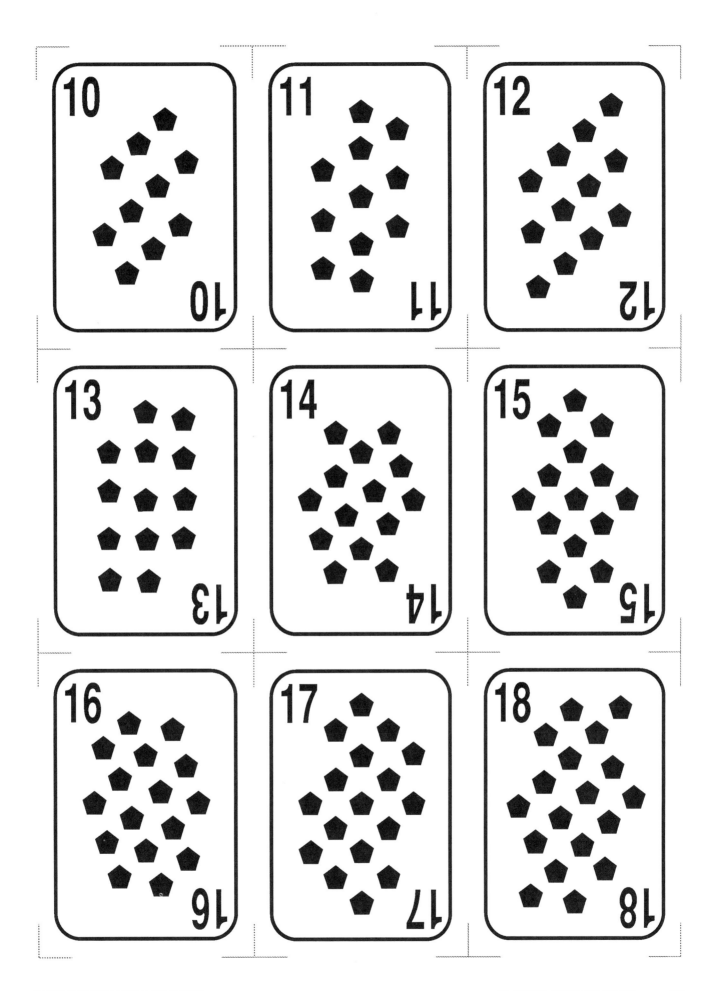

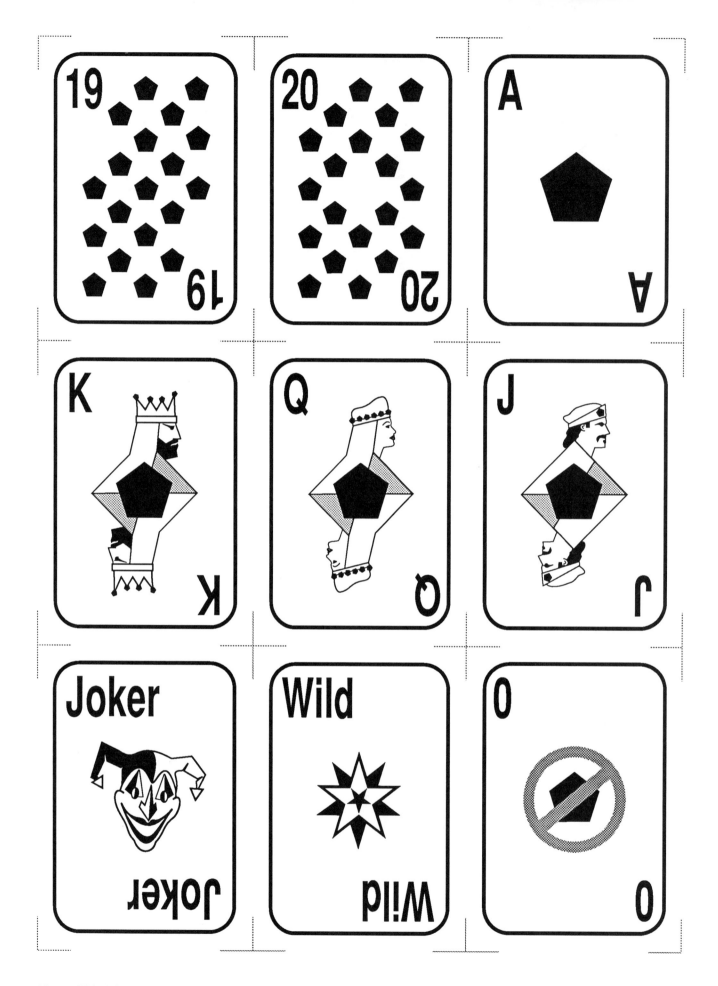

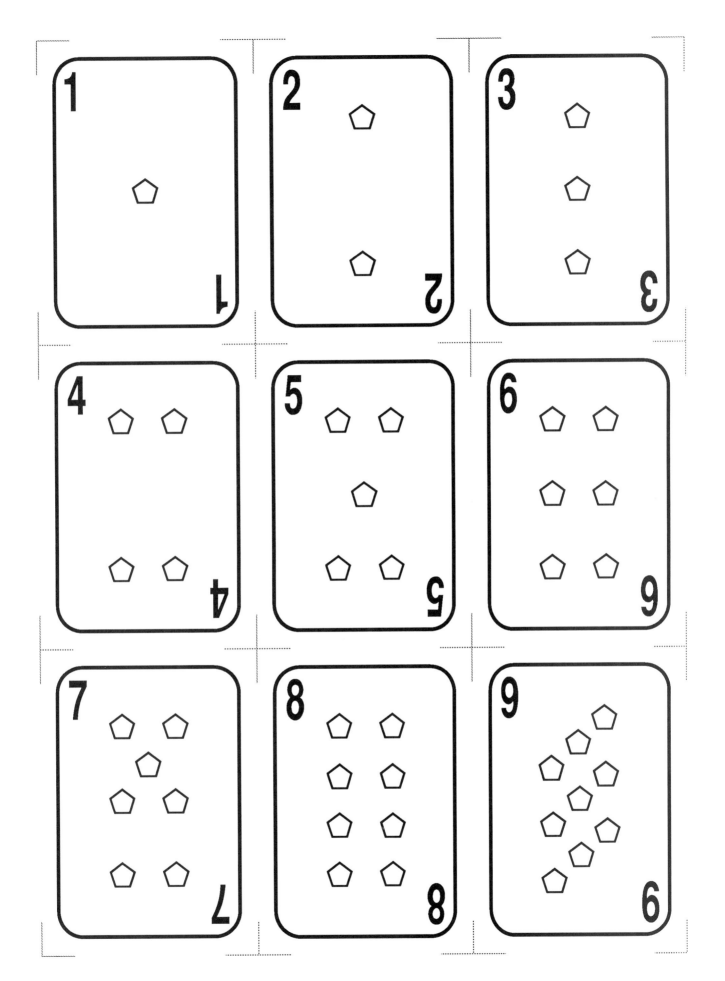

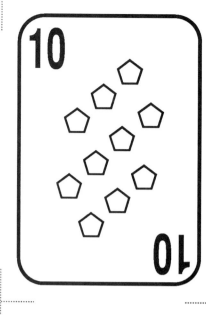
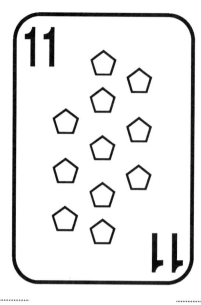

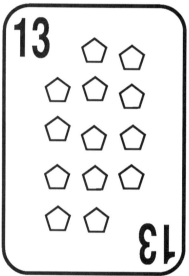
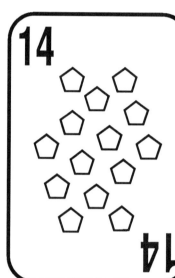

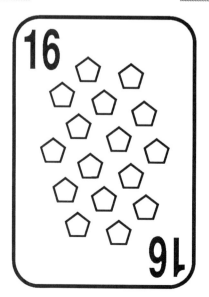
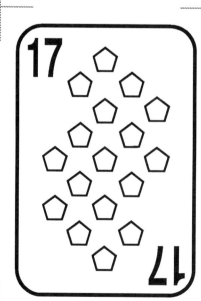
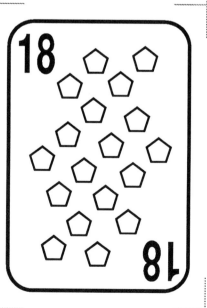

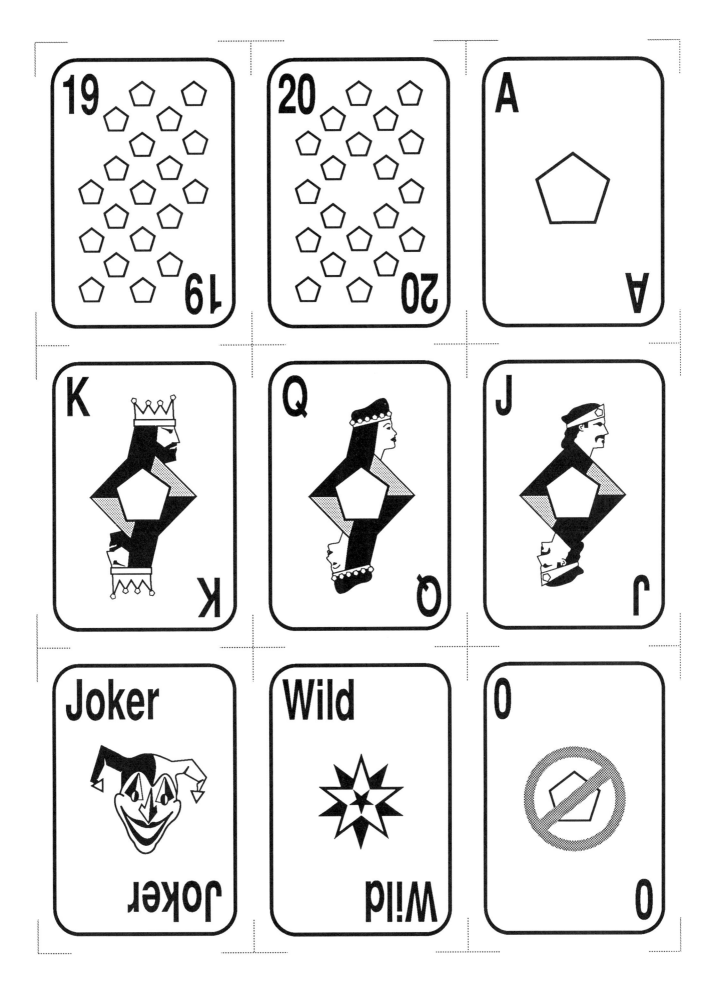

© Dale Seymour Publications

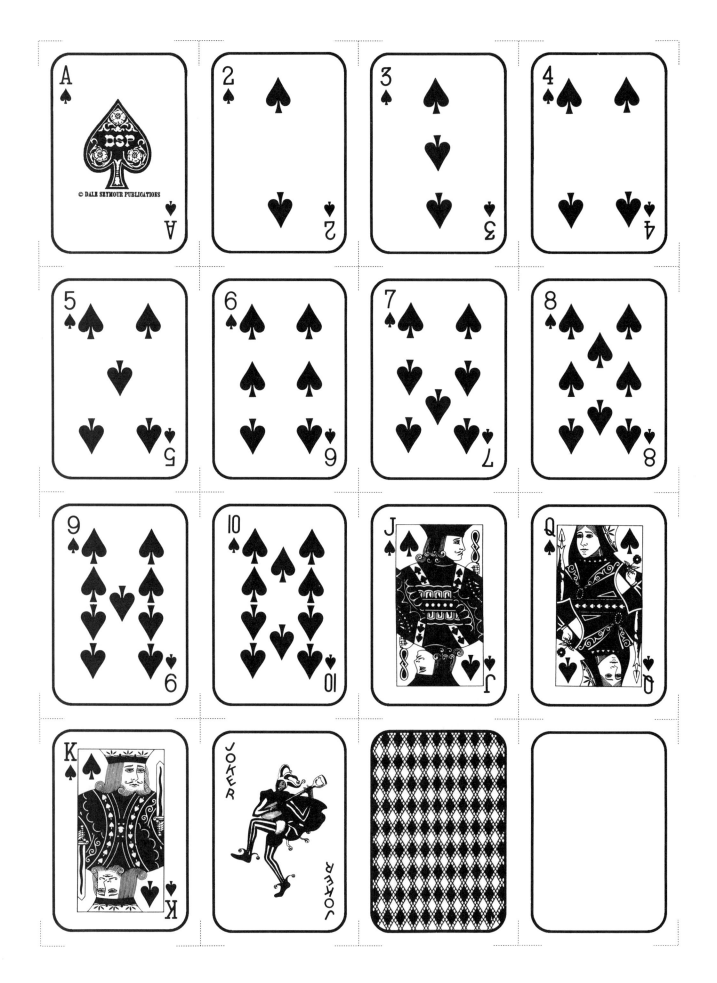

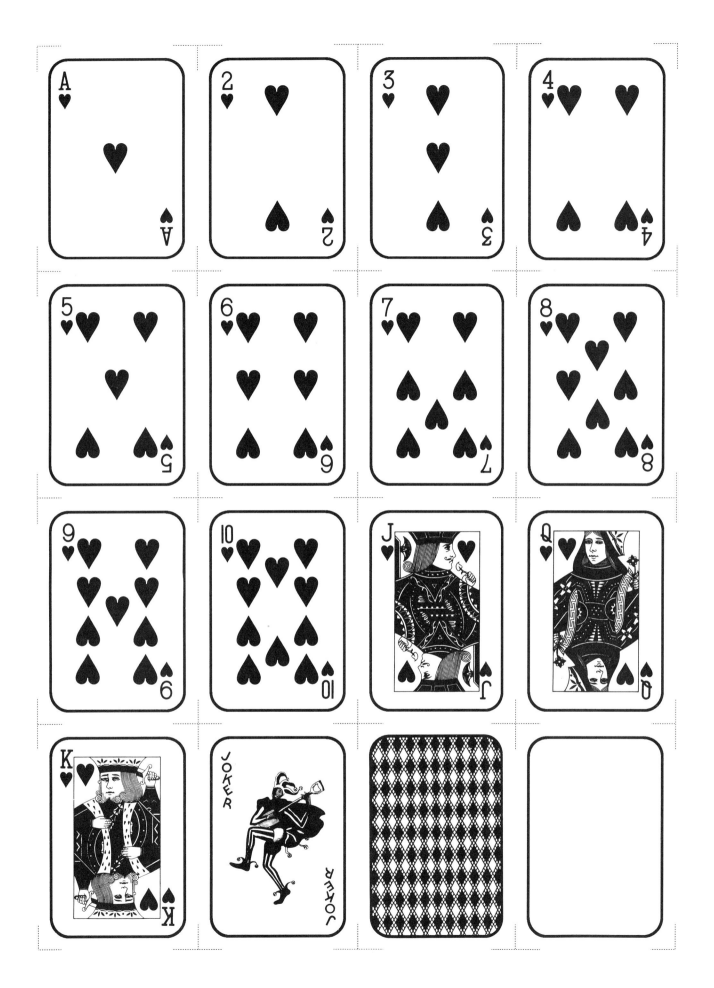

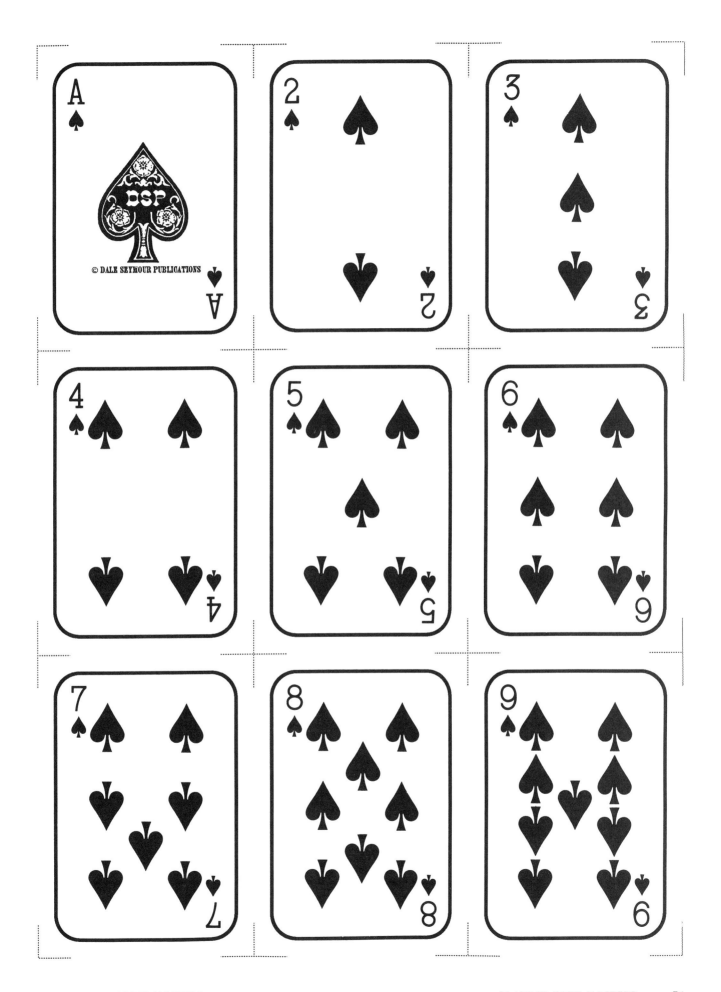

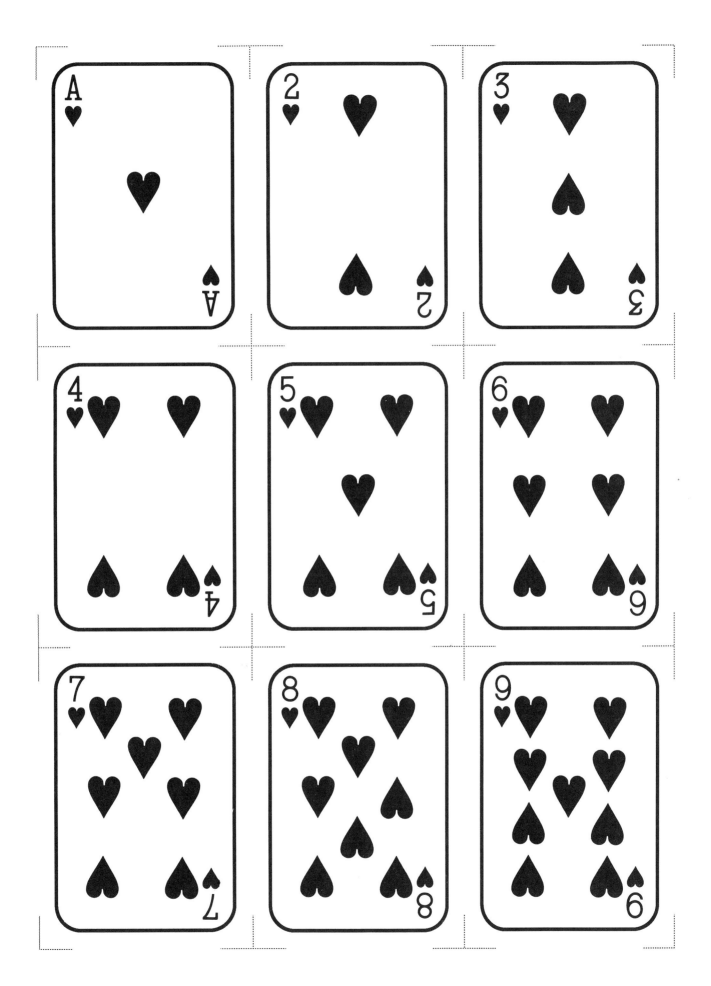

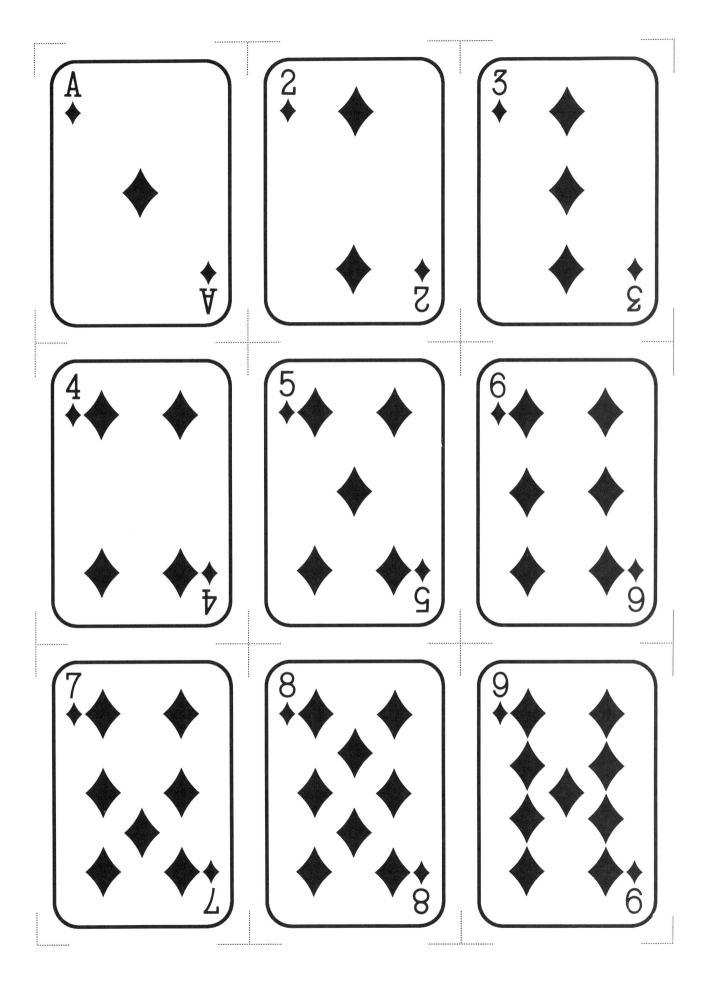

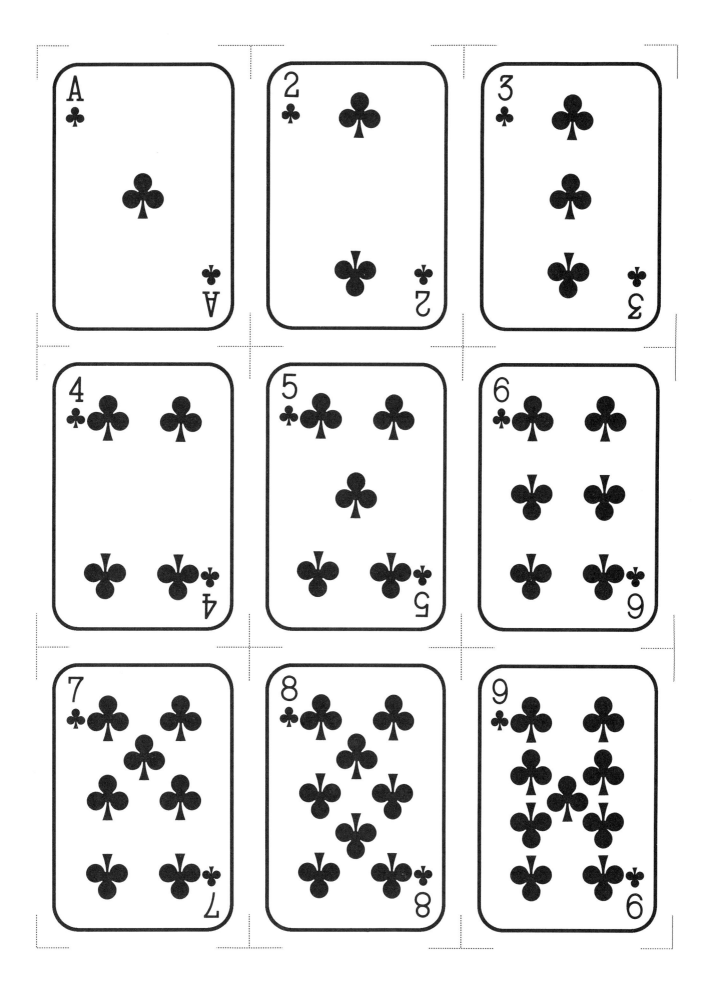

PROBABILITY MODEL MASTERS
© Dale Seymour Publications

Spinner Masters

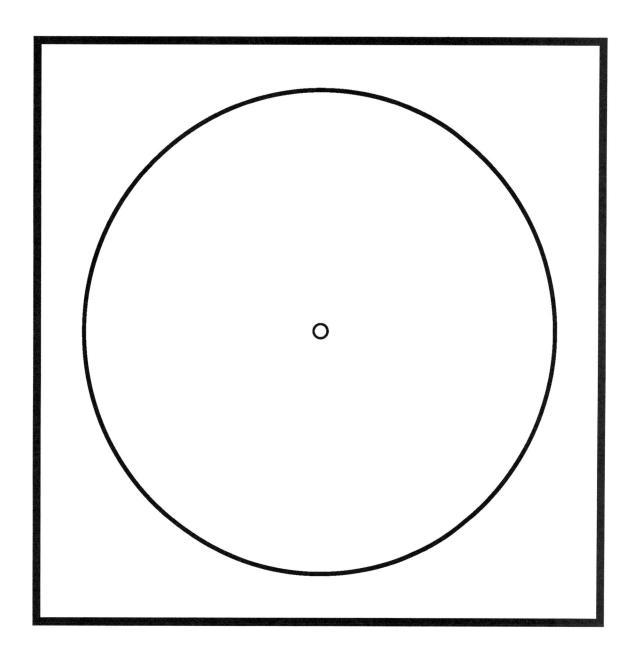

UNDIVIDED

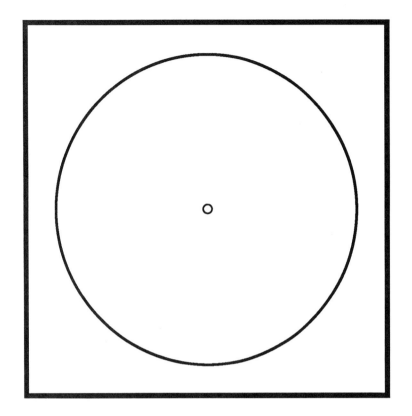

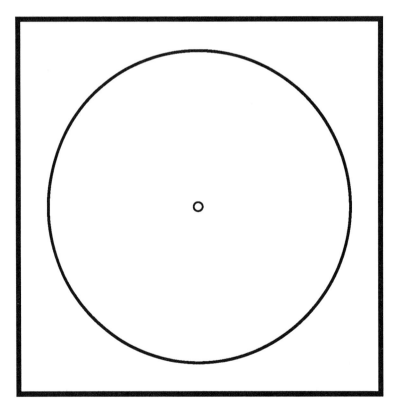

PROBABILITY MODEL MASTERS
© Dale Seymour Publications

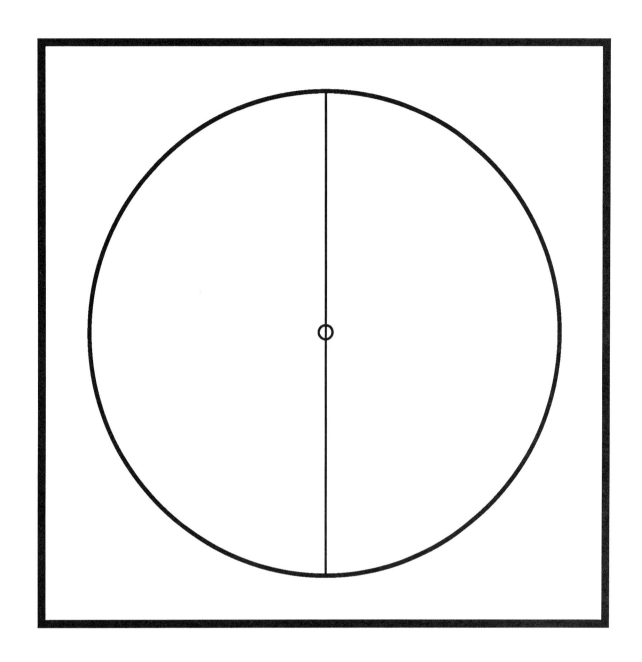

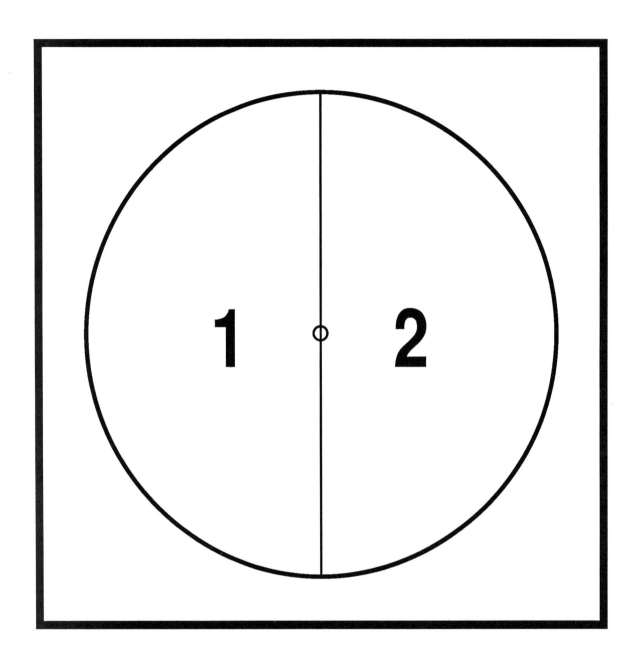

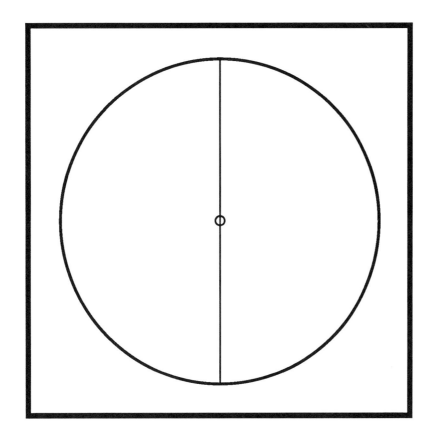

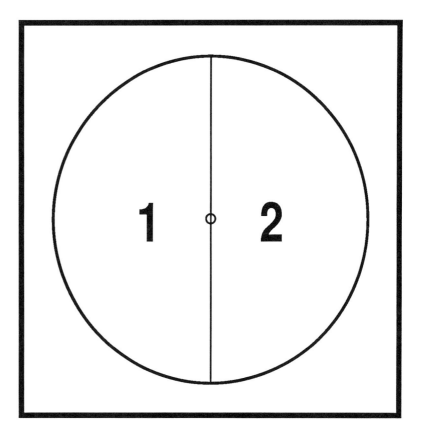

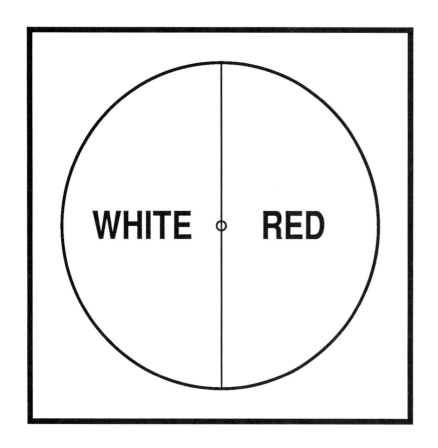

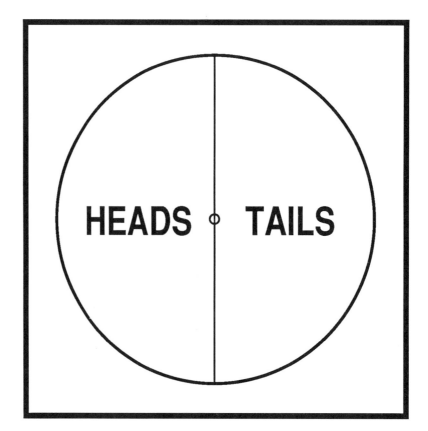

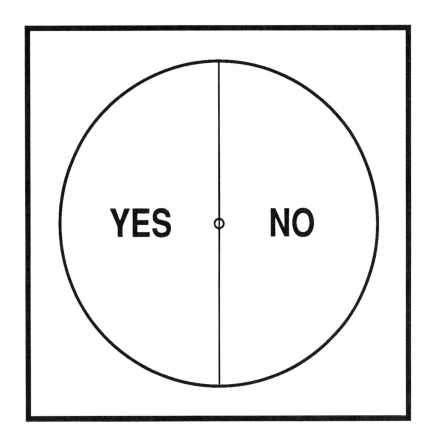

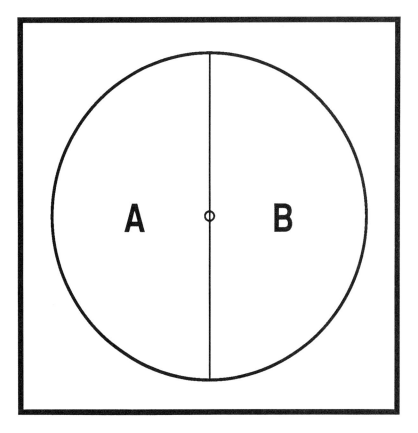

THREE SECTORS

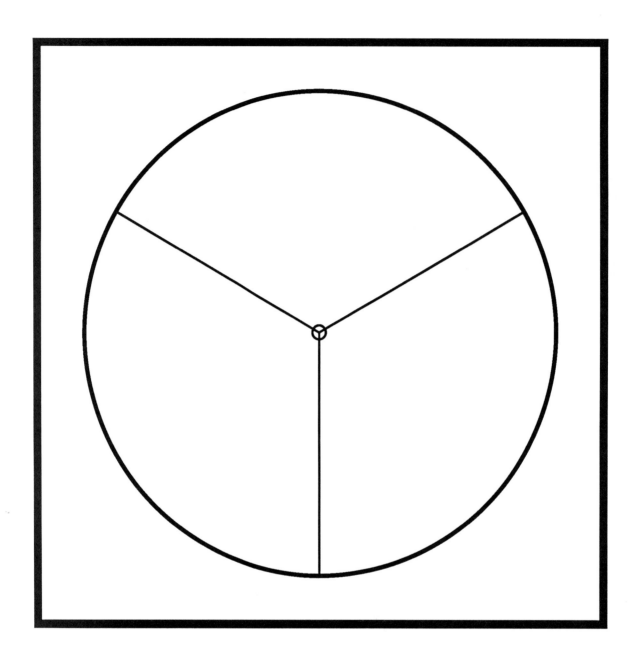

PROBABILITY MODEL MASTERS
© Dale Seymour Publications

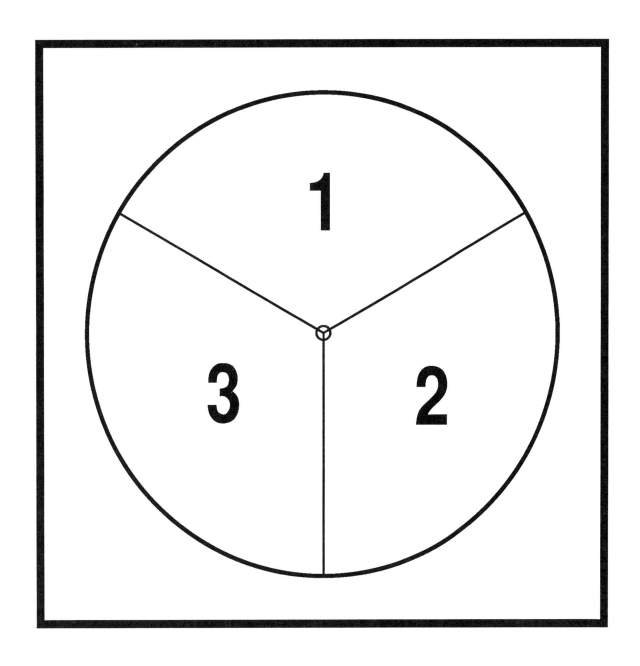

THREE SECTORS

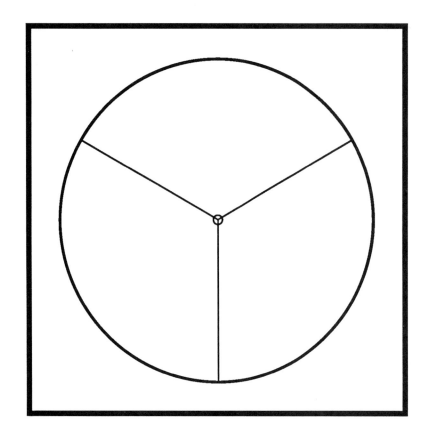

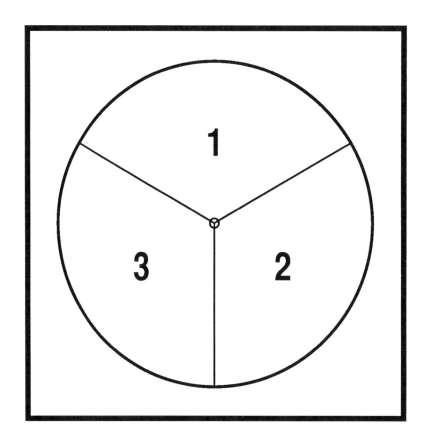

PROBABILITY MODEL MASTERS
© Dale Seymour Publications

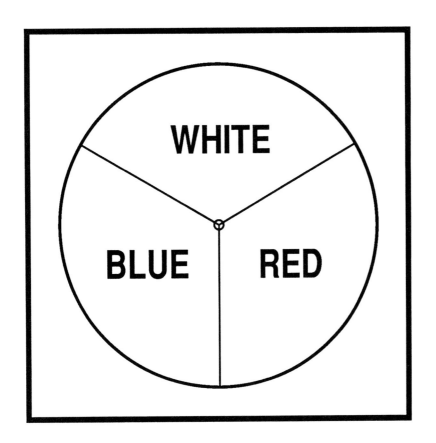

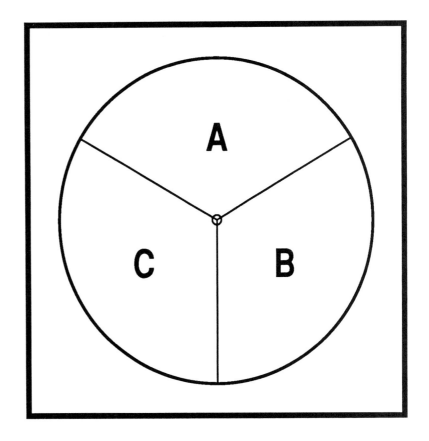

FOUR SECTORS

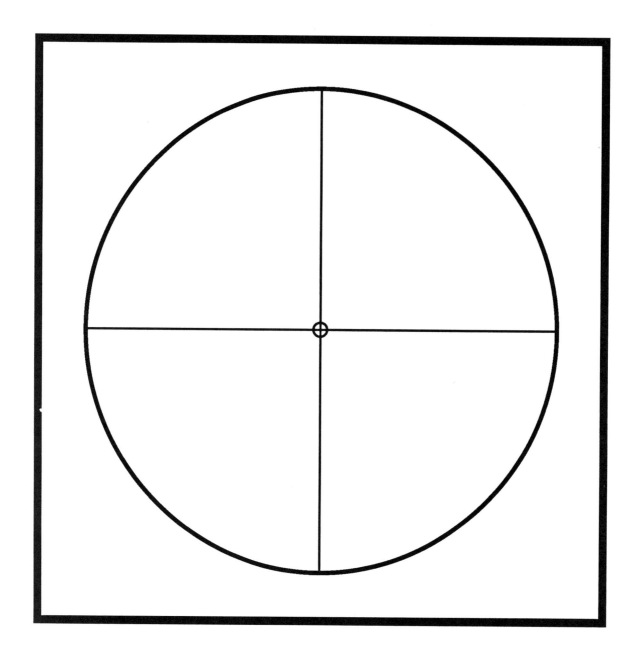

PROBABILITY MODEL MASTERS
© Dale Seymour Publications

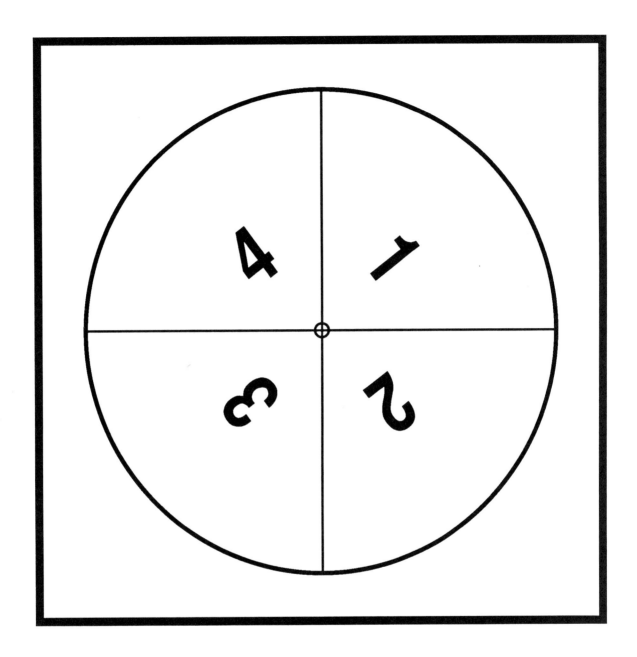

FOUR SECTORS

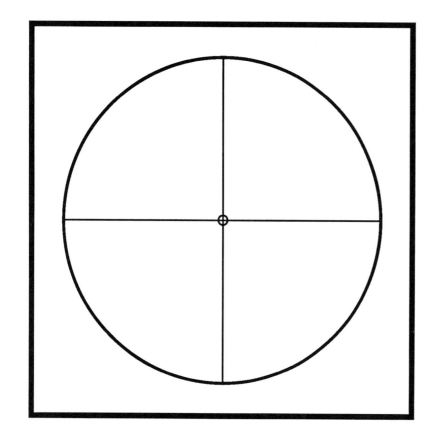

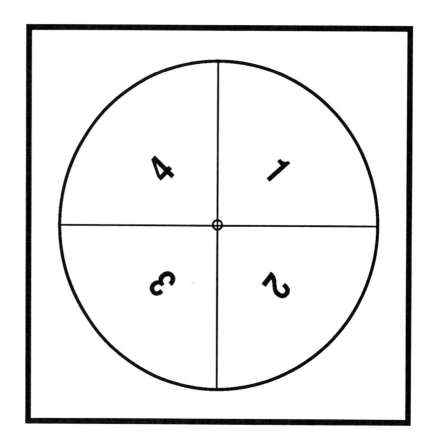

PROBABILITY MODEL MASTERS
© Dale Seymour Publications

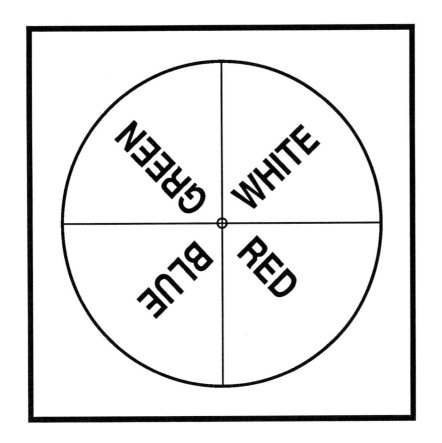

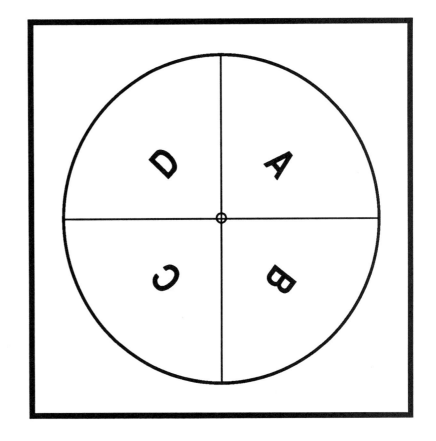

FIVE SECTORS

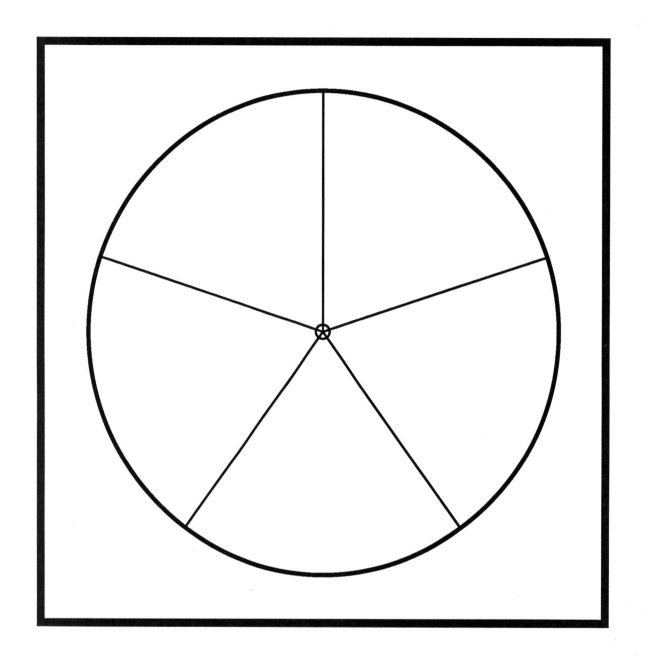

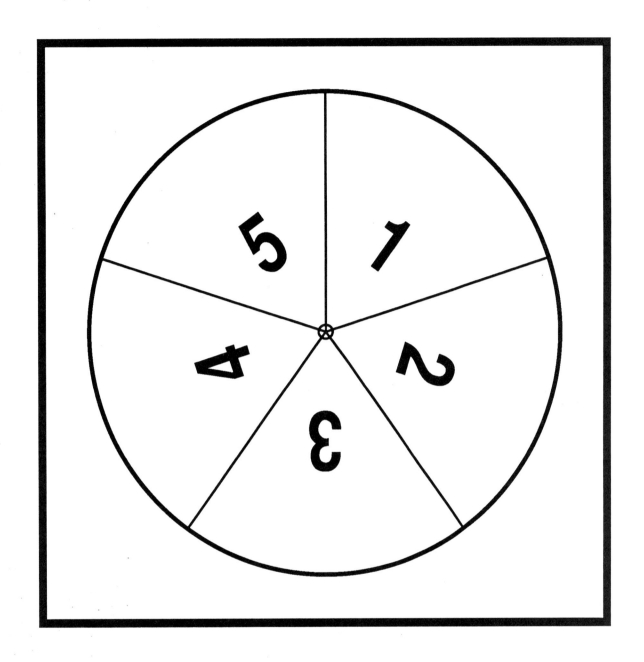

FIVE SECTORS

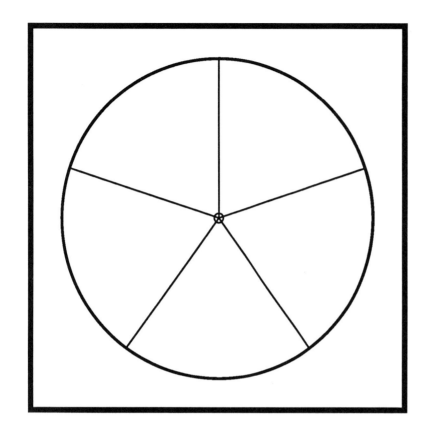

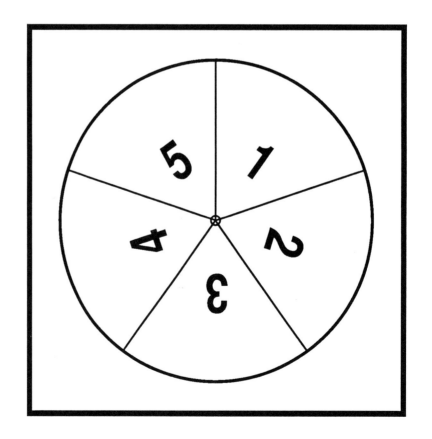

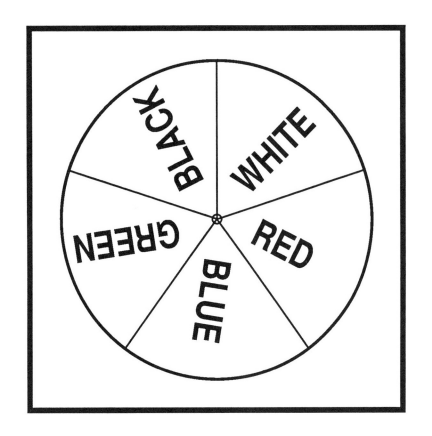

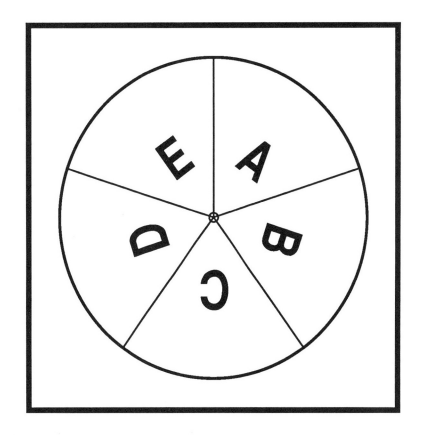

SIX SECTORS

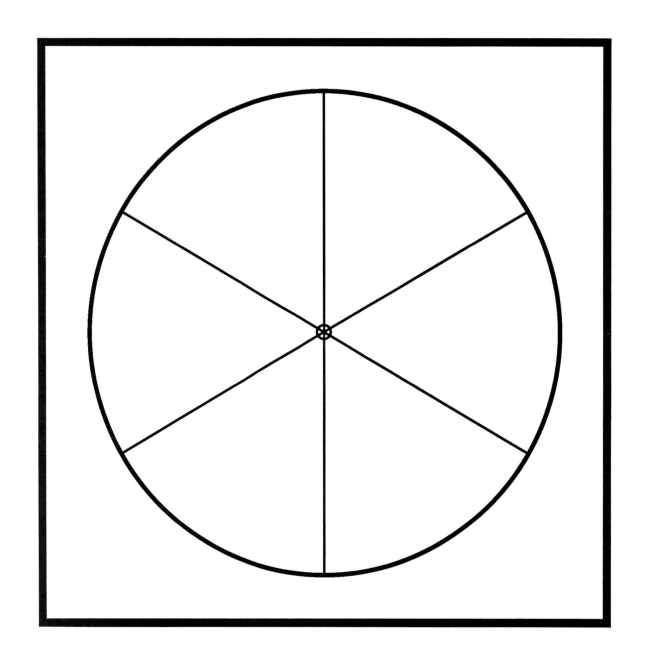

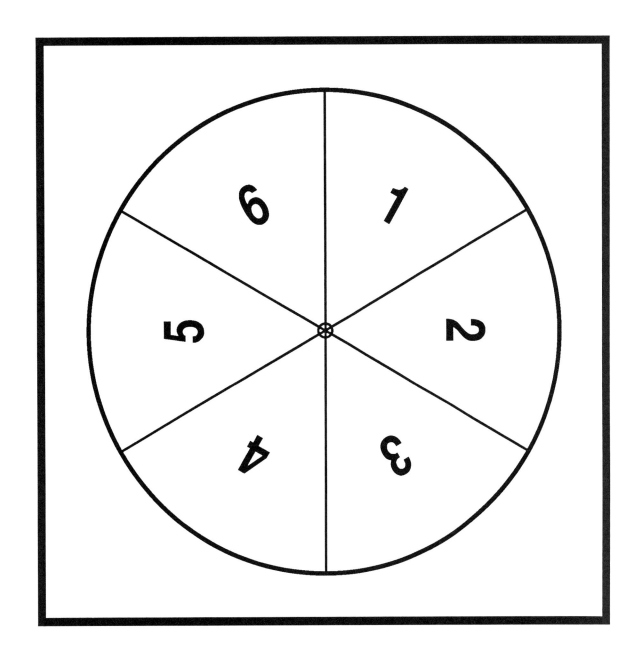

SIX SECTORS

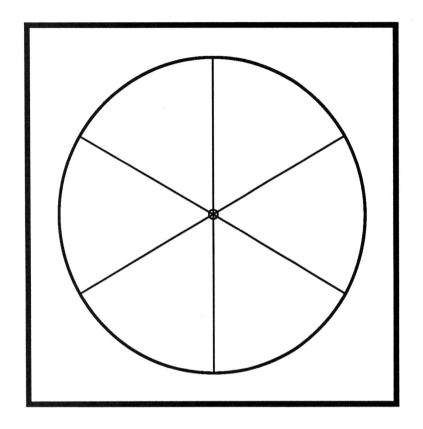

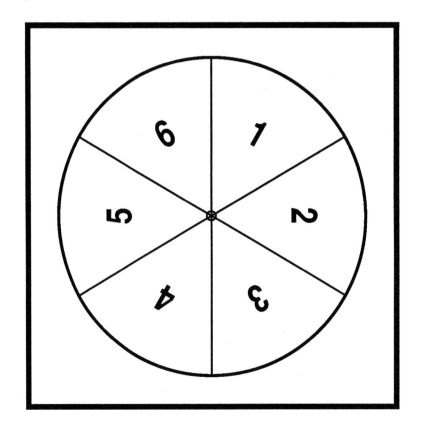

PROBABILITY MODEL MASTERS
© Dale Seymour Publications

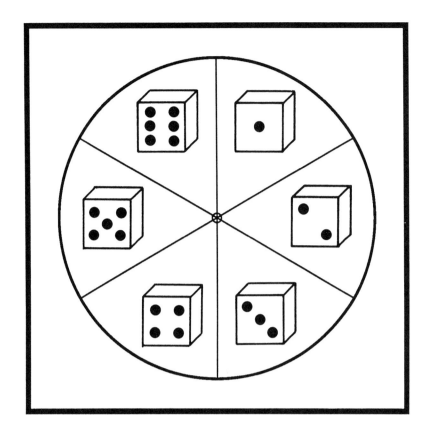

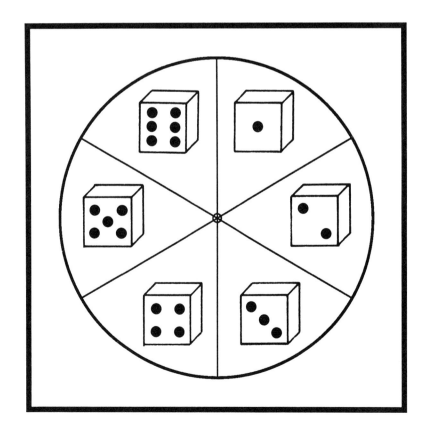

SIX SECTORS

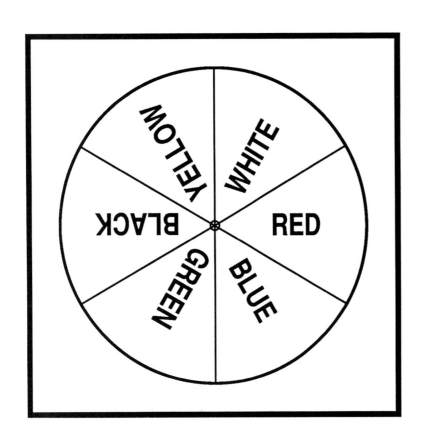

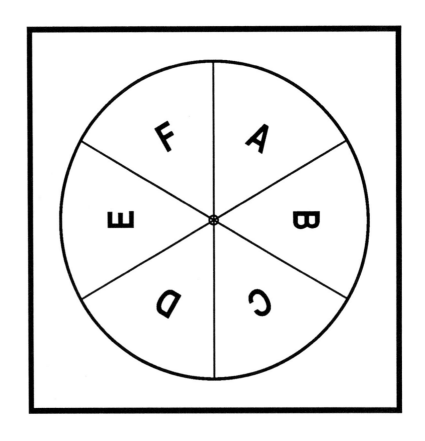

PROBABILITY MODEL MASTERS
© Dale Seymour Publications

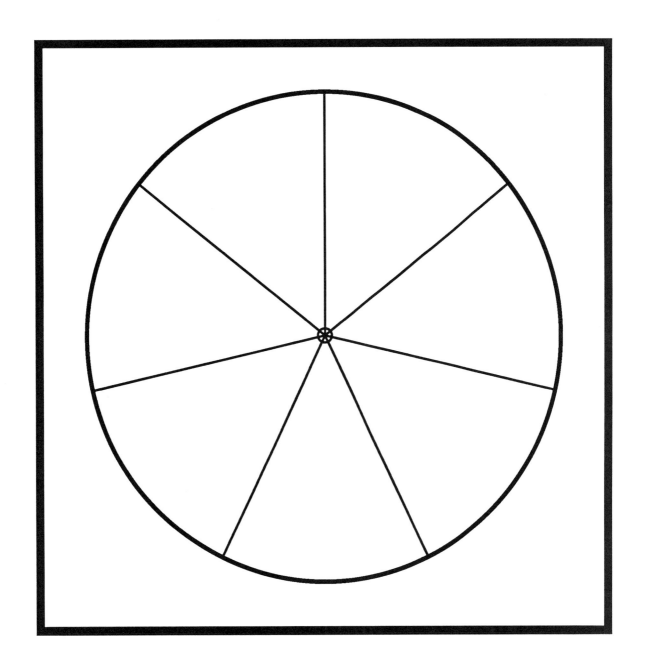

SEVEN SECTORS

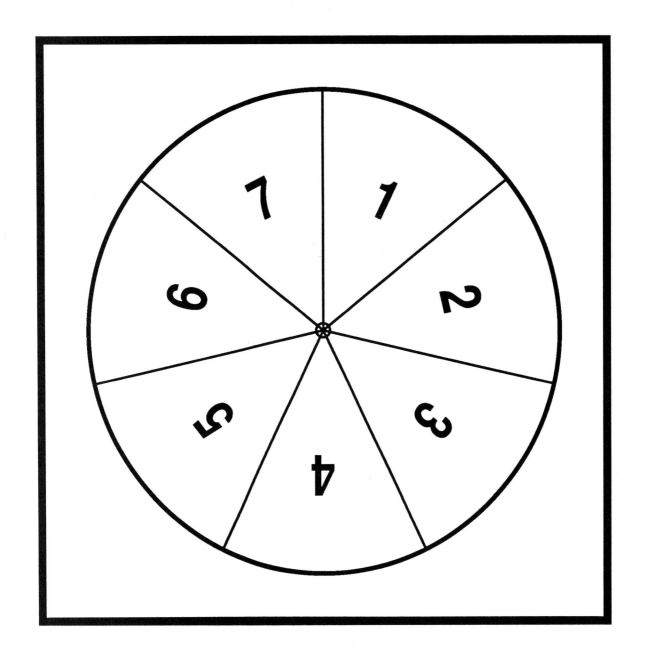

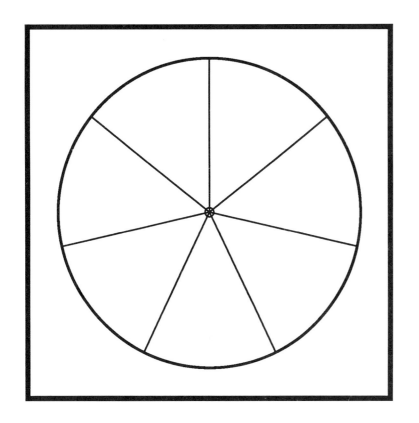

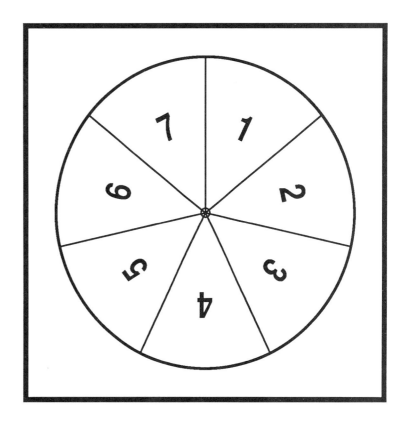

SEVEN SECTORS

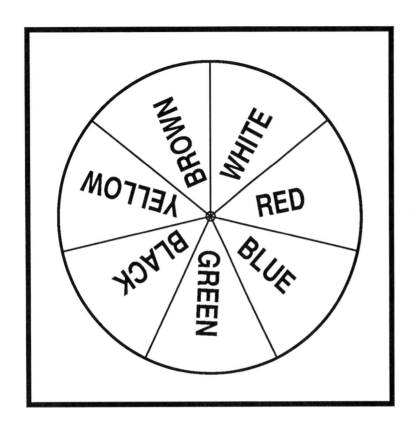

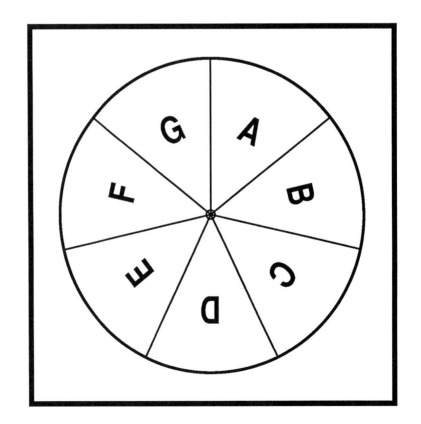

PROBABILITY MODEL MASTERS
© Dale Seymour Publications

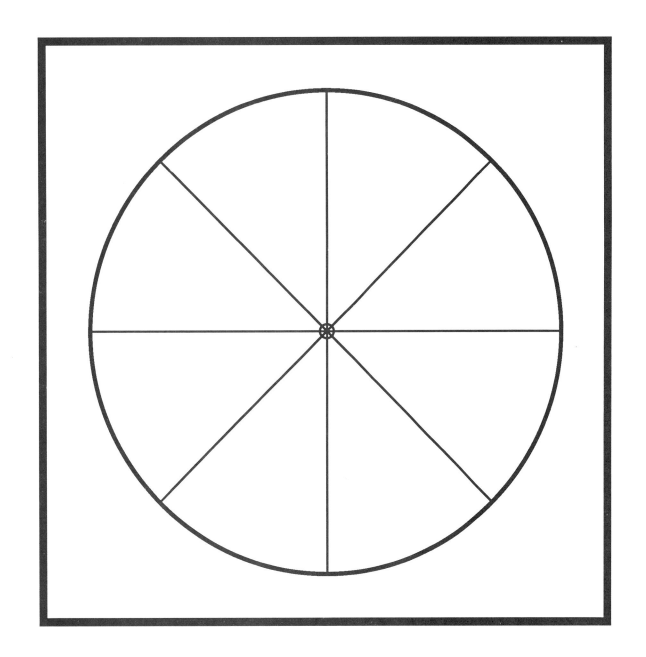

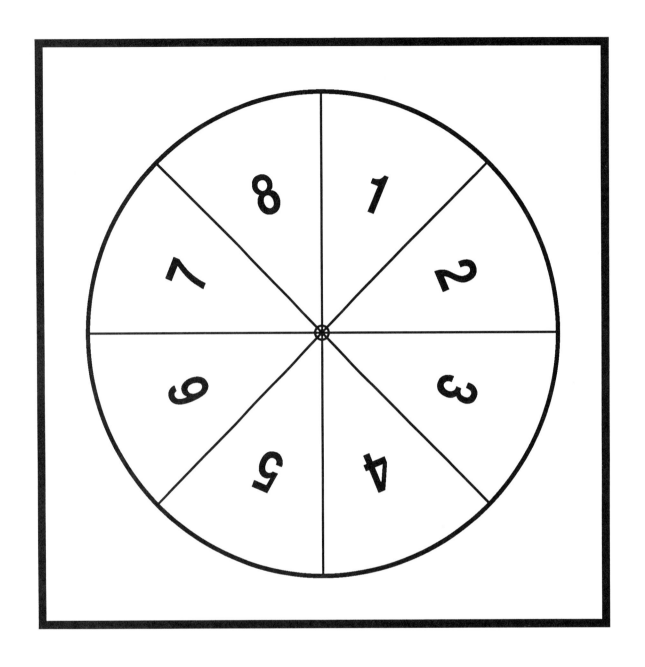

PROBABILITY MODEL MASTERS
© Dale Seymour Publications

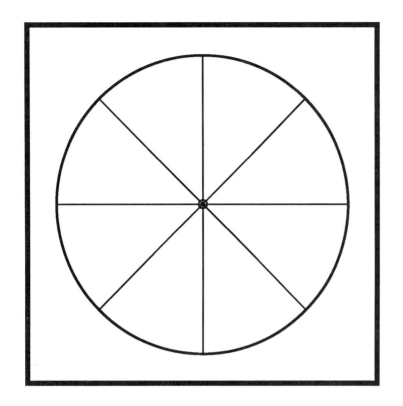

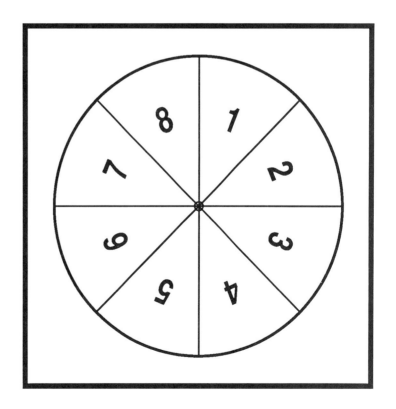

EIGHT SECTORS

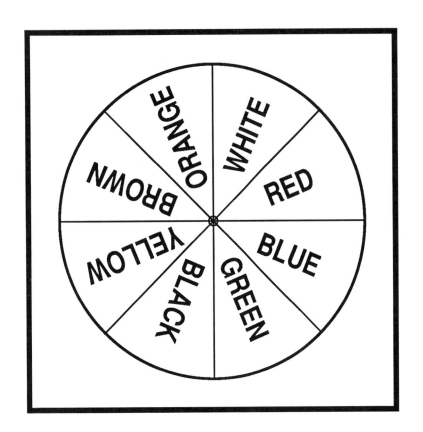

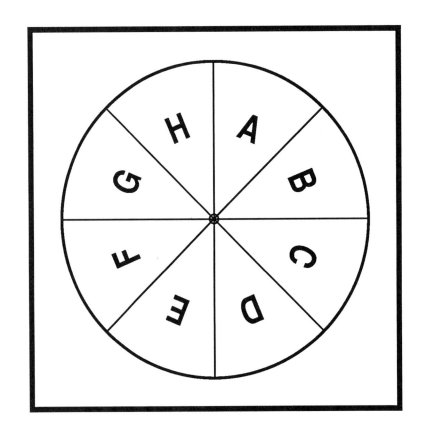

PROBABILITY MODEL MASTERS
© Dale Seymour Publications

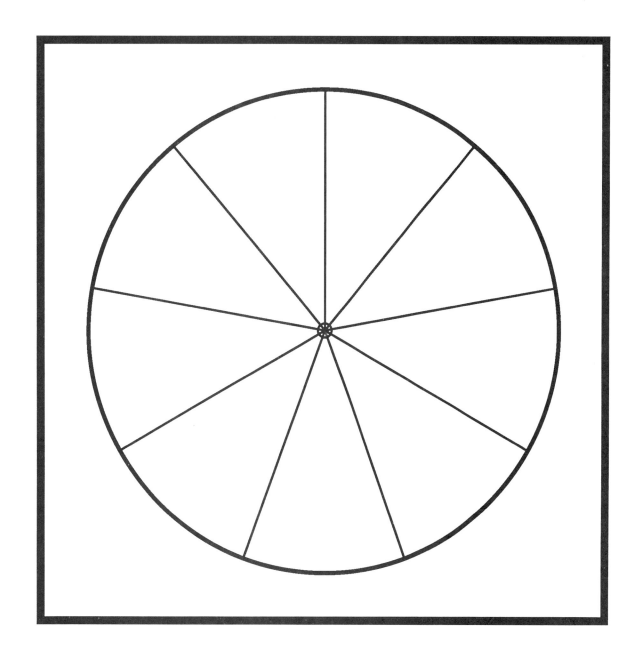

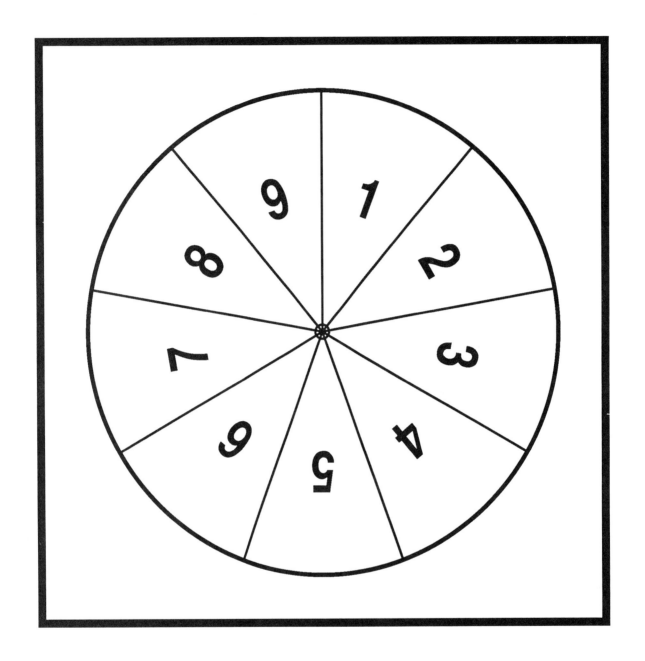

PROBABILITY MODEL MASTERS
© Dale Seymour Publications

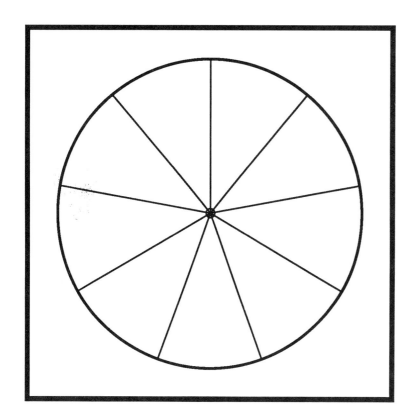

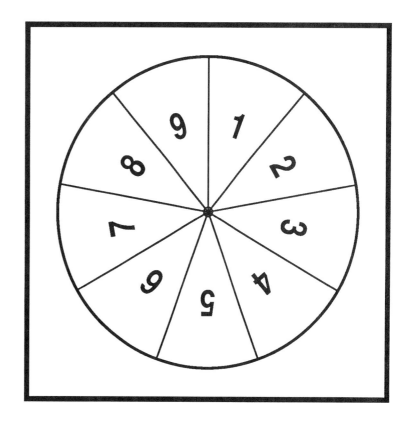

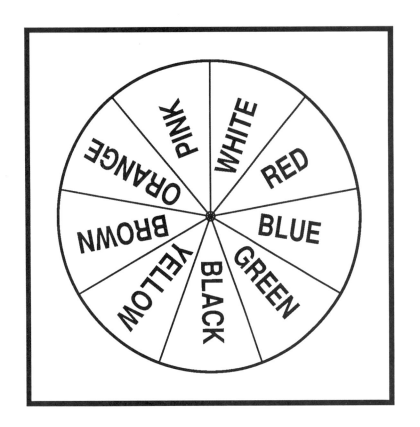

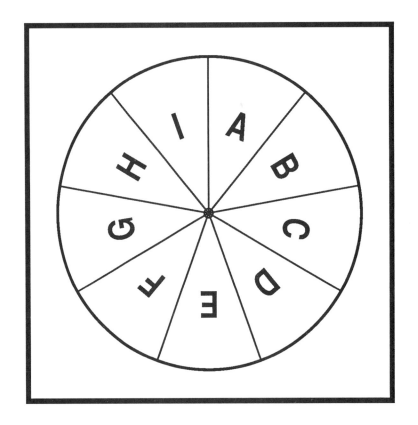

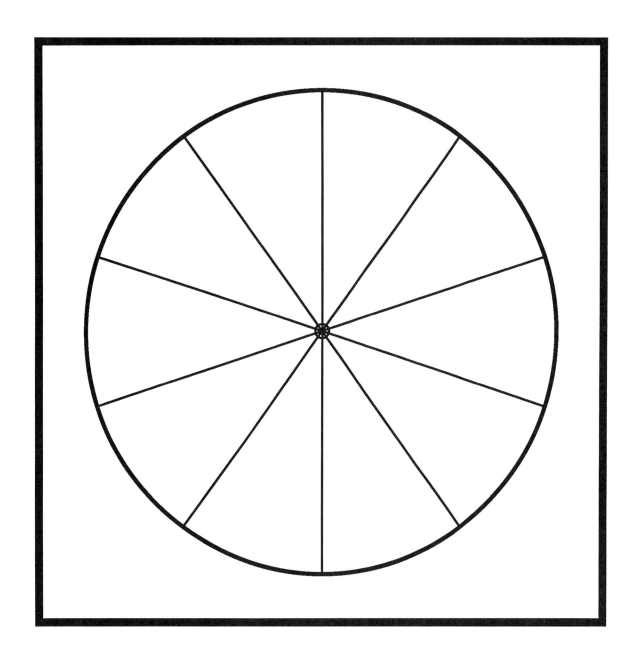

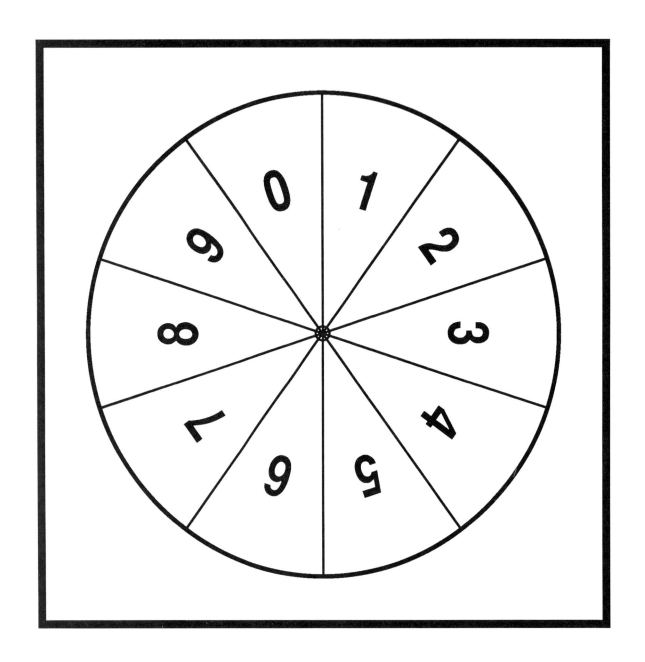

PROBABILITY MODEL MASTERS
© Dale Seymour Publications

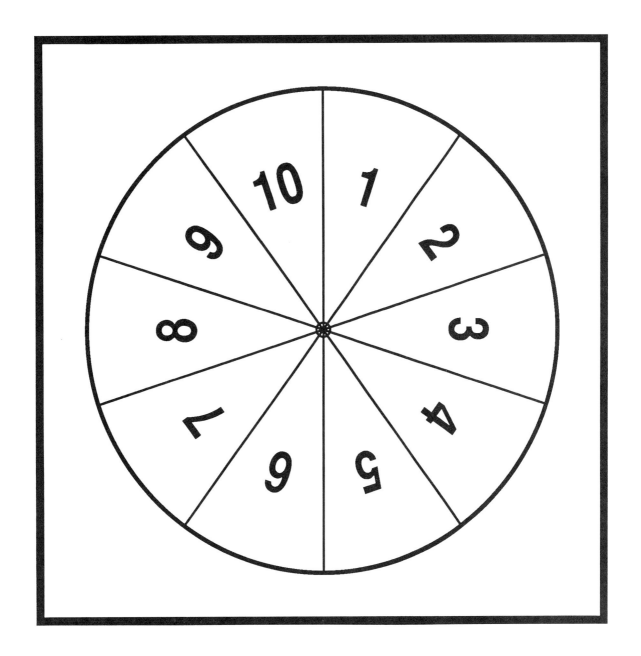

TEN SECTORS

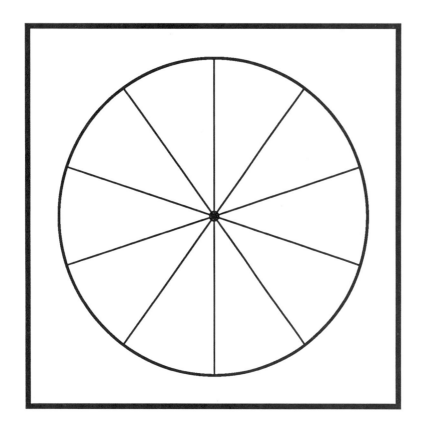

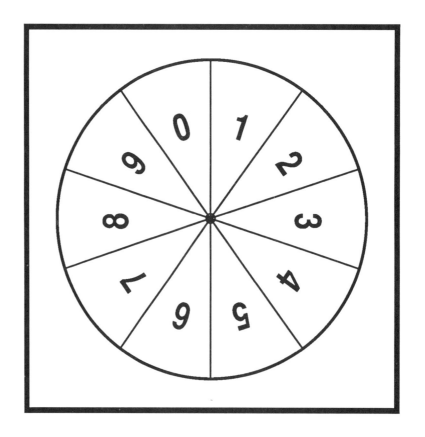

PROBABILITY MODEL MASTERS
© Dale Seymour Publications

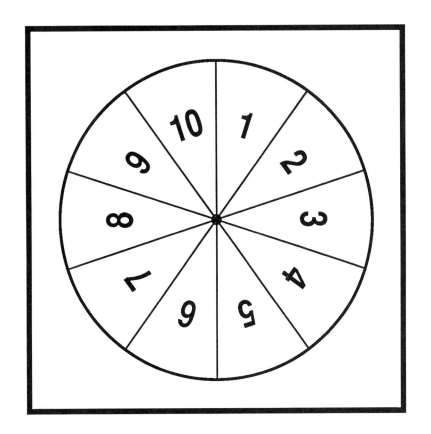

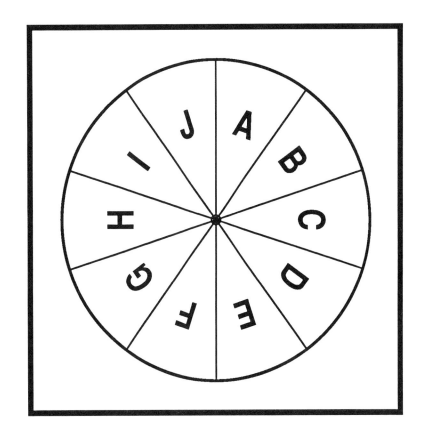

CIRCULAR PROTRACTOR

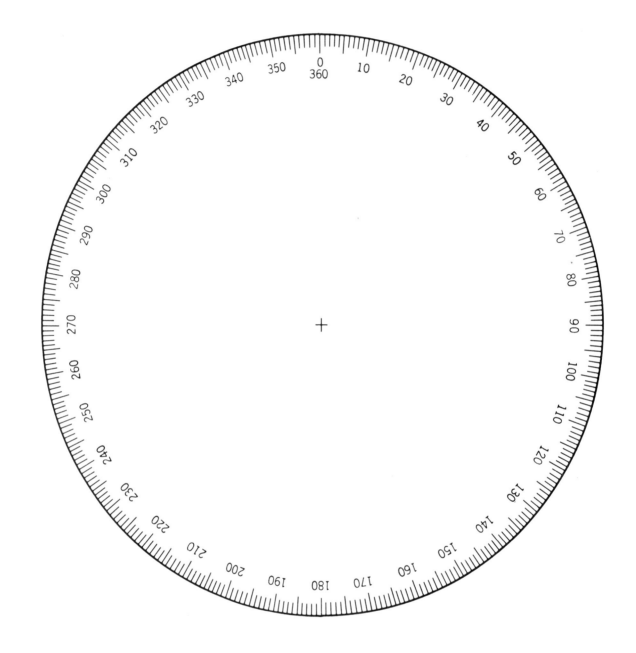

PROBABILITY MODEL MASTERS
© Dale Seymour Publications

Dice, Heads and Tails Cards, & Color Card Masters

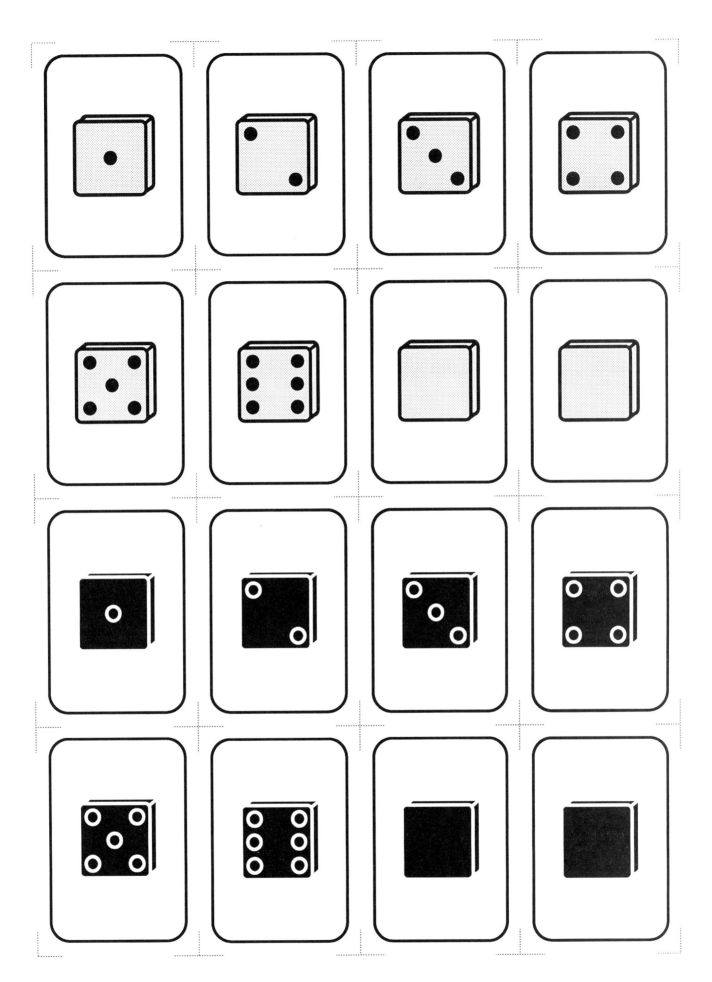

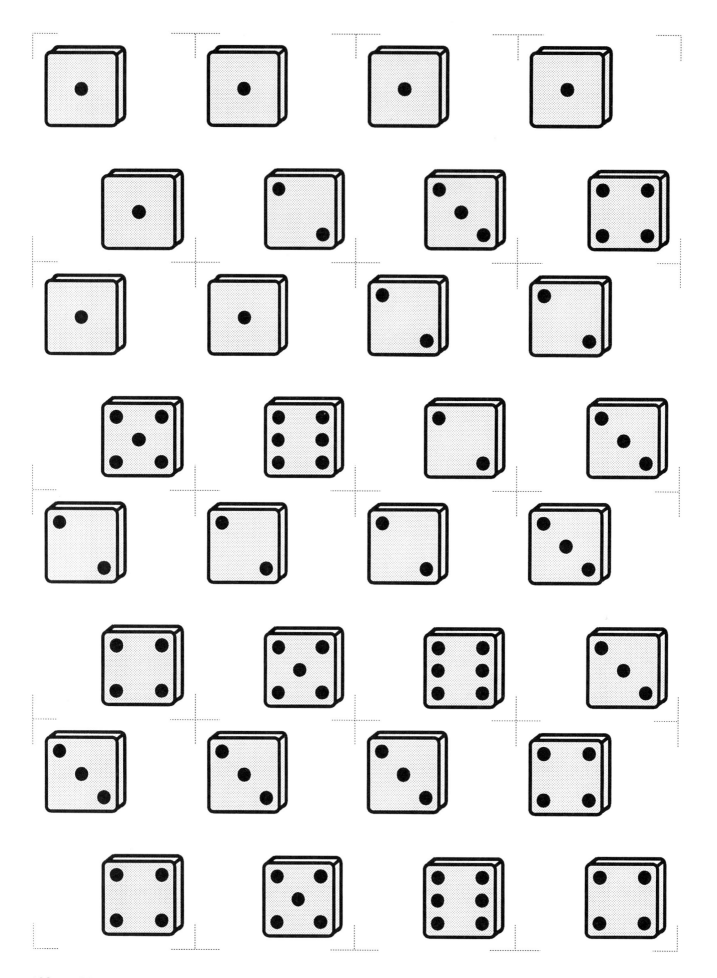

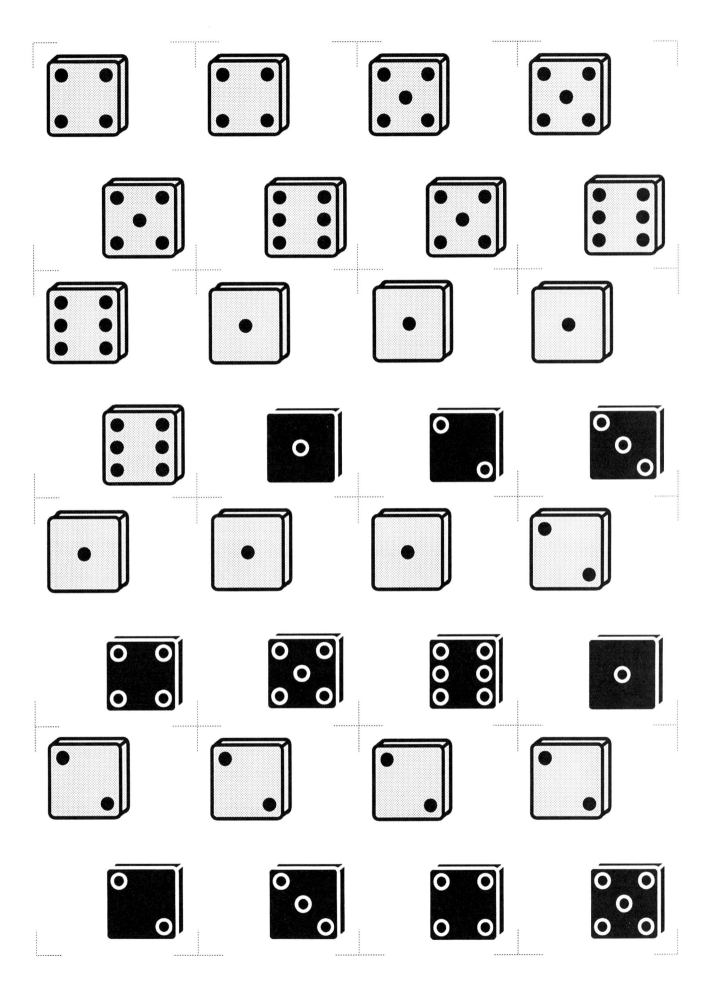

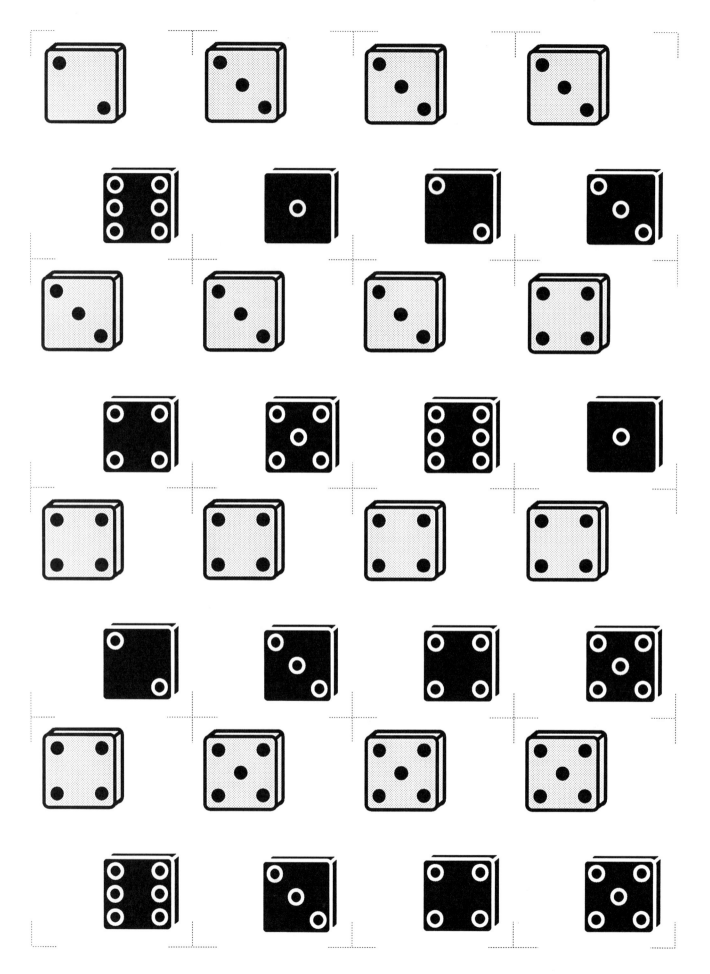

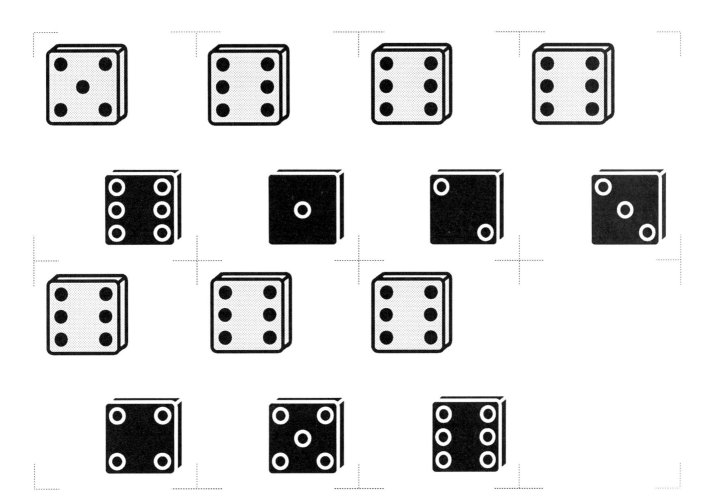

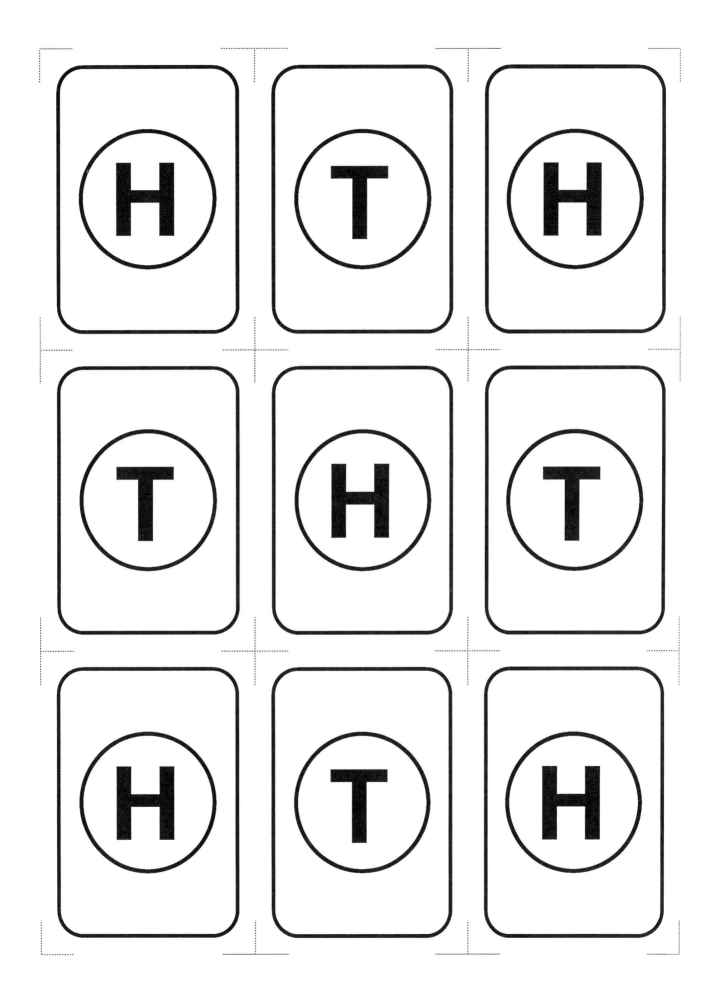

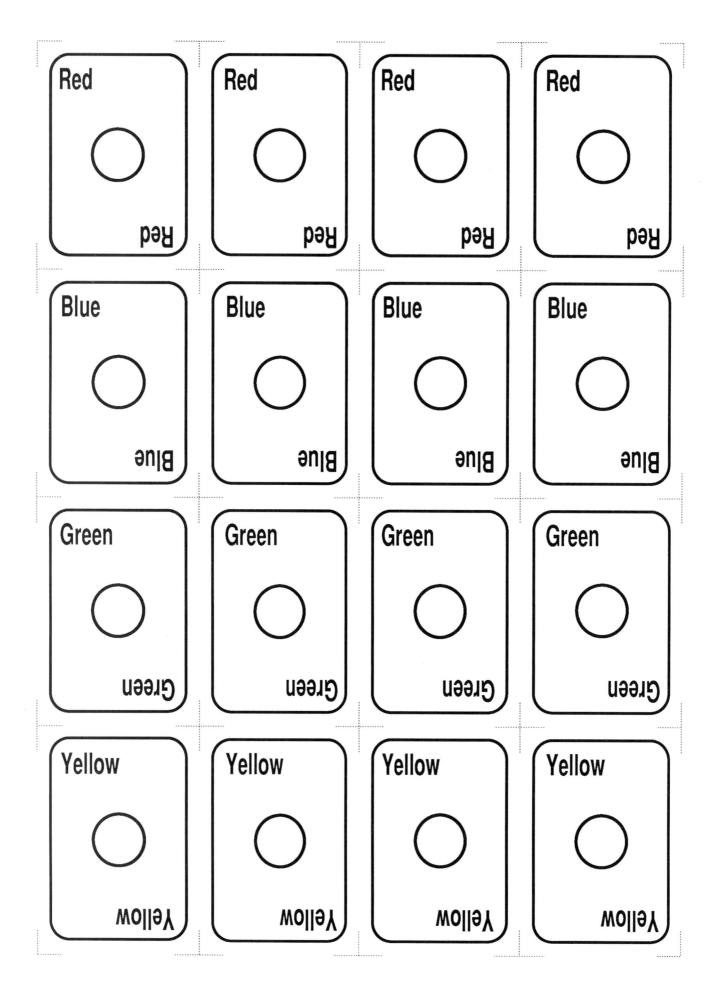

PROBABILITY MODEL MASTERS
© Dale Seymour Publications

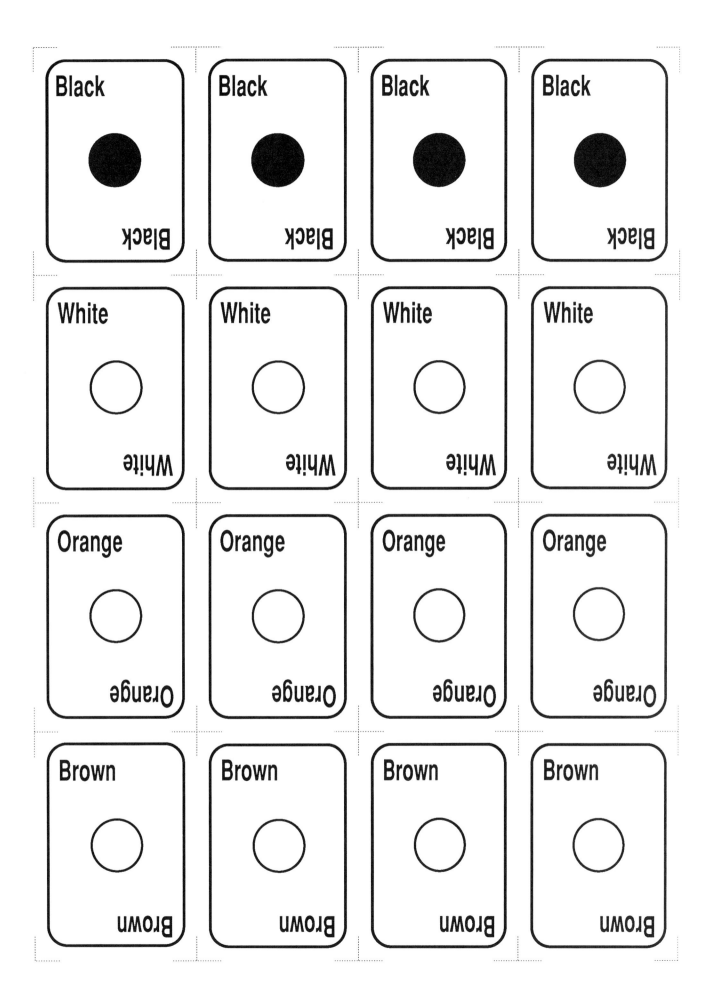

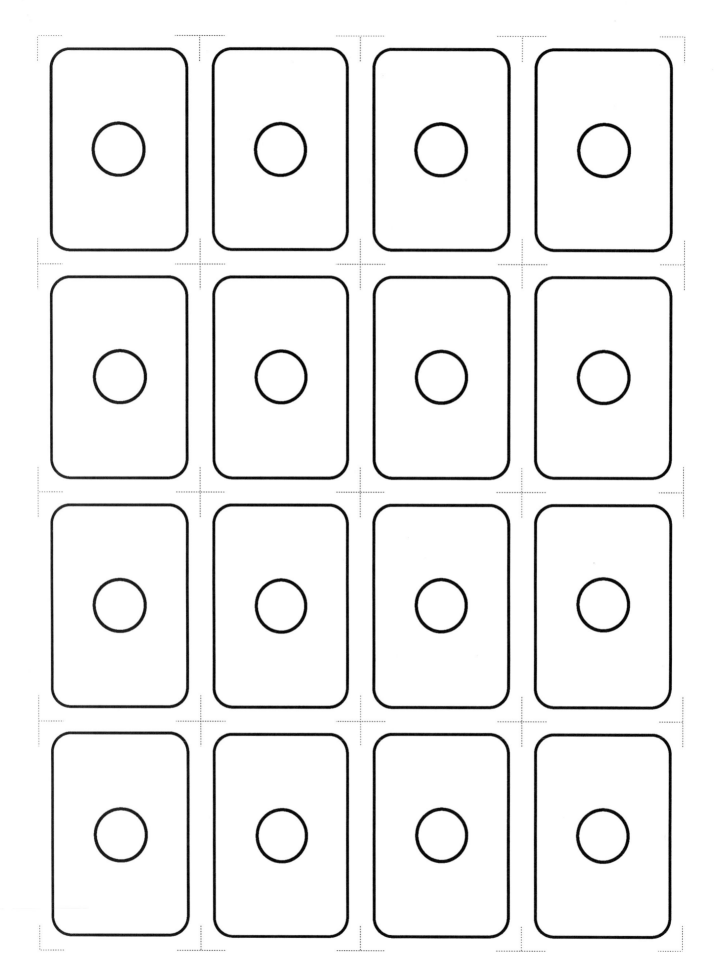

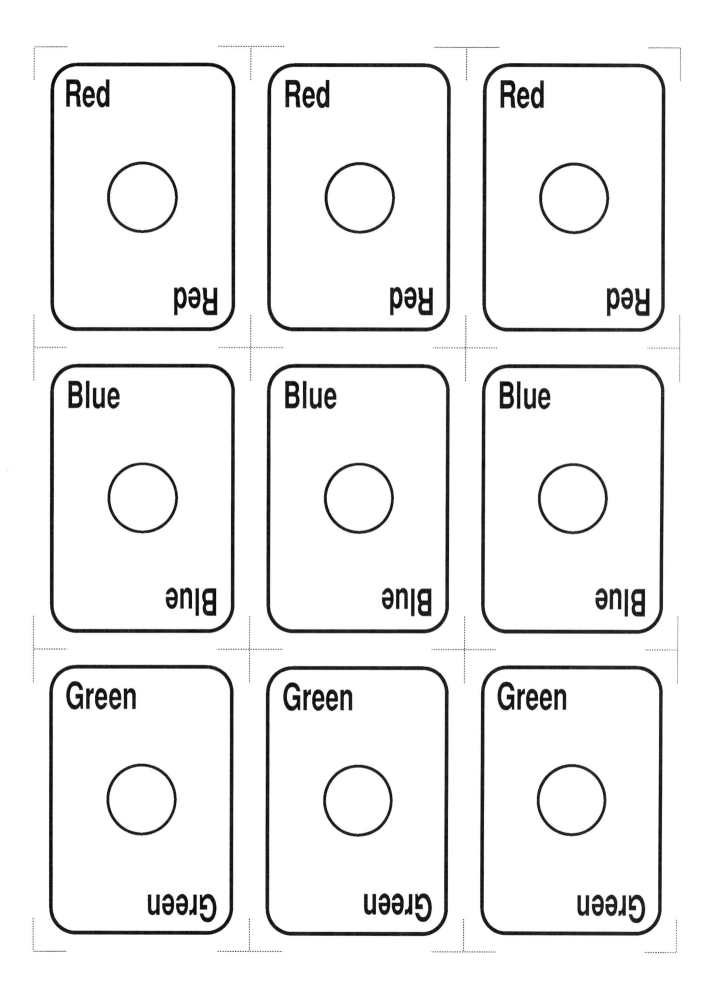

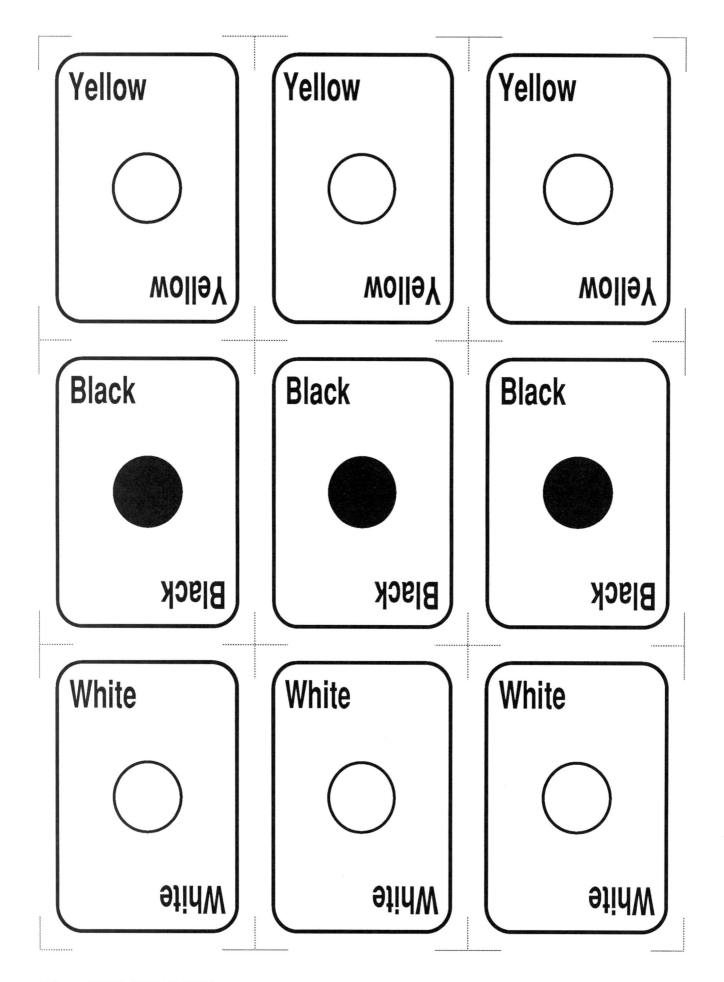